Notions from a Time of Peril

Other Books by
Glenn Alan Cheney

Thanksgiving: The Pilgrims' First Year in America

How a Nation Grieves: Press Accounts of the Death of Lincoln, the Hunt for Booth, and America in Mourning

Journey on the Estrada Real: Encounters in the Mountains of Brazil

Journey to Chernobyl: Encounters in a Radioactive Zone

Promised Land: a Nun's Struggle Against Landlessness, Lawlessness, Corruption, Slavery, and Environmental Devastation in Amazonia

His Hands of Earth: Courage, Compassion, Charisma, and the Missionary Sisters of the Sacred Heart of Jesus

Just a Bunch of Facts

Quilombo dos Palmares: Brazil's Lost Nation of Fugitive Slaves

Love and Death in the Kingdom of Swaziland

Acts of Ineffable Love

Neighborhood News

Frankenstein on the Cusp of Something

Passion in an Improper Place

Poems Askance

Law of the Jungle: Environmental Anarchy and the Tenharim People of Amazonia

Notions from a Time of Peril

Glenn Alan Cheney

NEW LONDON LIBRARIUM

Notions from a Time of Peril

by Glenn Alan Cheney

Published by
New London Librarium
Hanover, CT 06350
NLLibrarium.com

ISBNs

Paperback: 978-1-947074-54-5

Hardcover:978-1-947074-55-2

eBook: 978-1-947074-56-9

The essays in this book originally appeared in *The Day*, of New London, Conn., or its local subsidiary papers, the *Times*, between January 2020 and August 2021.

Contents

Nature

Big Ideas and Questionable Intents

Uncertain Times

On Stuff

Maybe It's Just Me

Looking Back

Little Bucket of Miscellany

Nature

The Joys of Meadow

Around this time of year, I'm glad to bid adieu to winter and welcome the season of gin and tonics in the yard. But then I think about the yard and then I think about the lawn and then I remember lawnmowers and the chore and noise of lawncare.

One solution to that particular summer chore: a lawnmower with a cupholder.

But there's a better solution. It's called a meadow.

Every lawn longs to be a meadow. That's why we mow them—to crush their dream, to cut them down to size, to flagellate them to conformity.

And we dump poison on them to kill their uppity dandelions. We cast chemicals upon them to make them grow faster so we can mow them more. We wage war on the moles and voles.

Why? Mainly to prove ourselves superior to nature and neighbors, as if we are what we mow.

I don't want to be what I mow. I want to be what I don't mow. I want to be the unmowed—a meadow.

Every yard has room for meadow. A meadow can be three feet across or the full length of a yard. Think of it as a lawn you don't need to mow or a garden you don't need to till, weed, or water. If you absolutely must establish your dominance, put a little fence around it. Then just leave it there, looking nice.

How nice? Well, just wait and see. Let it become what it becomes. Appreciate the special beauty of it—the shapes and hues of the grass, the way it drapes, the unexpected, unpredicted arrival of wildflowers—the same flowers you used to think of as evil weeds.

The word for those flowering weeds is "forbs." Local forbs include some of the prettiest names in all flowerdom: baby blue eyes, shirley poppy, gloriosa daisy, candytuft, baby's breath, love in a mist and sweet william.

You can buy such seeds or just wait until they find their way to your meadow. Your meadow becomes a garden of its own making. The longer you let your meadow be—months, years—the more your forbs.

And the more your forbs, the more your fauna. Yes, insects, of course, but so what? If they like meadow, they stay in meadow. And then your meadow becomes a bird feeder. The birds bring beauty and music.

Did you know that you can buy recordings of birdsong? But you can't buy recordings of lawnmower song. That's something to think about while you're sitting near your meadow, nursing your G&T, watching your meadow grow as you listen to your unenlightened neighbor mow her unenlightened lawn.

Here's something else you might not know: Yard irrigation accounts for a third of all residential water use, a national average of nine billion gallons a day. And half of it evaporates or runs off unused because lawns aren't especially good at sucking up water. You want water sucked up, get a meadow.

Another fun fact: America has 63,000 square miles of lawn—roughly 13 times the size of Connecticut. Turf is the most widespread irrigated crop in the country.

And yet another: 25 percent of Democrats, but only 16 percent of Republicans, say lawn moving is their least favorite chore. One out of five Americans would prefer to shovel snow.

And another: Each weekend, 54 million Americans mow their lawns, burning 800 million gallons of gas. According to the EPA, American mowists spill more gas in a year than the Exxon Valdez spilled into the Gulf of Alaska.

And another: one lawnmower operating for an hour produces more volatile organic compounds (e.g. carbon dioxide) and nitrogen oxides (the stuff of smog) as 11 new cars driving for an hour.

I know what you're thinking: deer ticks. You think they're coming to get you. Well they're not. They like a shady, humid area of tall vegetation. Ticks don't pursue. They wait. Sure, they might like a meadow—if deer take them there—but there ain't no tick alive who's going to leave a meadow to come looking for you.

And if you're still scared, mow a band of lawn around your meadow. It doesn't have to be much. Ticks are tiny. They can't walk far. A little lawn's a lightyear to them.

So this summer, do yourself—and your world—a favor. Plant yourself a meadow. Then go plant yourself near the meadow. Watch it grow and change. Appreciate it. Sip your gin and appreciate what you're not doing.

Summer's Symphony

Quick question: How long can summer's honey breath hold out against the wrackful siege of battering days?

Please don't answer that. I don't want to think about it. I don't want to know. Not yet.

I want to hear birds singing the morning out of the night, bullfrogs bemoaning their loneliness, the silence down deep in a lake. I want to smell honeysuckle and sassafras. I want to lie in meadow grass and think about blue.

I don't want to cringe at the sting of cold every time I step out the door. I don't want to feel trepidation at every weather report. I don't want to wonder if this year, yet again, the trees will manage to push pale new leaves from their stiff, bare limbs.

They did it again this year, but how? I've never heard a good explanation. I've heard about meristems and axils, the phloem, parenchyma and xylem, the hypha and mycorrhiza. If I keep asking, "Yeah, but why?", the explanation eventually comes down to "the trees just know…"

I think it's nice that trees know. They know what to do and when to do it without being remanded to their rooms for misbehavior or sent to college as soon as they're old enough to bear fruit. Even an acorn knows what to do.

I just like the notion of trees knowing. It's astonishing that for all our post-modern sophistication, we still refer to things knowing. Stock markets know. Computers know. Cars know. Mother Earth knows. Dumb luck knows. My heart knows.

(I'm not so sure about my computer. I think it only thinks it knows, but for all I know, it's just playing dumb. Why isn't there an un-dumb button?)

God only knows how a butterfly knows when it's time to fly to Mexico. How does distant snow know when I've put away my snow shovel? How did it know that this year I waited until the Fourth of July?

And then there's "they." I don't even know who "they" is, but I know they know. They know where I live. They know how old I am. They know how old my refrigerator is, and they have my credit card number. I fear the day will come when they will just up and send me a new fridge because they figure I'm too dumb to know I need an upgrade.

The day will come when UPS delivers me a coffin I never ordered. I'm going to open the box and think, "I knew it..."

But I don't think they know how long summer's honey breath can hold out. I don't think they even care. I bet they're already planning Columbus Day sales and warming up the Christmas jingles.

I'm not waiting for winter or that grim UPS truck. While it's still warm in the evening, I'm taking my canoe across the lake and up the stream on the other side to beach on a rock below the rapids. As the last of the sun dies in the west, I'm going to listen to the birds chatter their good-nights in the twilight, then the frogs cranking up their mournful chorus from the mud.

And then the lone thrush, the last to sleep. Deep in the pillared dark, its lonely tootle flows, almost like a call to come in to the dark and the woes.

I'll take the heat. It's fine with me. I prefer a fan over A/C, a breeze over a chill. Easy for me to say, of course, because I'm too smart to wear a suit and tie in the summer. I don't earn squat for income, but I'm successful enough that I can work with my shirt off.

My theory: It's good to be hot in the summer. When autumn flares and yellow leaves shake against the cold, it's a relief. It feels good to snuggle into a sweater and take a breath of cold air. And when you look out the window and see that first snow carefully everywhere descending, it's beautiful. It's peaceful. It's good.

The Decent Way to Go

Imagine a better way to go into eternity...

Rather than have your organic compounds sealed in a box in a vault, you could become part of the ecosystem that has sustained you since before your birth. You could become the nutrients of new life. You could become a tree in sunshine, a home to birds and squirrels, a source of oxygen, that stuff you loved so much while living. You could join the ecosystem that sustains everyone you left behind.

Being buried without preservatives, without a casket varnished against rot, without a steel or concrete vault, is not a new idea. It's the way we did it for millennia. People who were born into nature were returned to it. What went around came around. Life went on.

Today we have a special term for this: green burial. People opt to have their bodies returned to earth with the intent of living again. No embalming. No casket unless of untreated wood. No vault. Just the body laid to rest in the earth.

Green burial is legal, yet it's rarely done. Why? Because few cemeteries accept green burials. In all of New England, only two cemeteries have sections for green burials, and not one is reserved for them exclusively.

Elizabeth Foley, an emergency room nurse formerly with Lawrence + Memorial Hospital, is going to change that. She has formed a nonprofit organization, Connecticut Green Burial Grounds, and as soon as she's arranged some acreage, people of organic tendency will be able to rest in true peace. Foley's plan goes one step beyond burial. She's going to have a tree planted over each grave. Before passing on, people (or their survivors) can choose an appropriate tree. Maybe an oak to symbolize strength, or a maple for elegance, or a monumental sycamore, perhaps a weeping willow.

(Sorry. No palm trees for snowbirds coming home to roost. It has to be a species native to Connecticut.)

Whatever the tree, it will inevitably take up the nutrients of the person buried below. Death becomes life. The deceased rise up as a tree. Loved ones can see that living thing, gather in the shade of it, touch it, maybe take home an acorn or a leaf.Little by little, the cemetery becomes a forest — a place of life that sustains itself with little or no maintenance. To those of environmental consciousness, a forest of trees, wildflowers, birds, butterflies, and other creatures is far more beautiful than a lawn that needs to be mowed and weed-whacked in perpetuity.

Foley says CGBG is finding no shortage of people wishing to be buried this way. What the organization needs is some land. Her desire is to find the right place somewhere in Eastern Connecticut. Why here? Because environmentally, it's a way to preserve land and nature. Economically, it's a source of employment as visitors come from far and wide for a decent burial. Historically, it's the way we used to bury people; and the way we someday will again.

Green burials are the only decent way to go. And green burial grounds are ideal for our region. We have the land. We appreciate nature. We appreciate peace. And frankly, we could use the business. We can only hope we have a green burial ground here, close to home before it's too late.

Election Day Screech

Always striving to defend democracy, I spent August 11 working the poll during the primary election. As a Deputy Registrar of Voters, I kind of had to be there from 5:00 in the morning until voting ended all the ballots—in-person and absentee—were sorted, counted twice, and sealed up, all the paperwork filled out and duly signed, all the ducks in a row, all the booths, tabulators, tables, papers, posters, accoutrement and equipment picked up, folded up, packed up, stacked up, and locked up.

The primary was a long, dull trudge toward a predestined conclusion. It was also a bumpy trudge. Under the pressures of the pandemic, rules were unclear, often flawed and in flux even as the voting was happening. The tabulator jammed with humid ballots. The sanitation was constant, the masks stifling.

The poll workers were diligent. The voters were great. No arguments. No issues. Workers worked together. Voters braved the heat, did their duty, and went back into the heat. Once again, democracy prevailed over anarchy.

The process may have been predestined, but it was also a dry run. We hit a few bumps. We had to hit them to know them. The bumps weren't roadkill. They were glitches—inevitable under the circumstances and solvable with cooperation and good intentions. We're gong to do this again on a smoother road in November.

I had coffee for breakfast, a parsimonious grinder for lunch, cold pizza for dinner, luke warm water all day. I got home around 9:30. I mixed myself a drink and went out to sit on the deck and look at the dark of the woods over the Little River. It was good. As E.B. White said, the sweetest sound in the world is "the tinkling of ice at twilight."

I'll say the same for the tinkling of ice a couple hours after the poll closes, especially with hushed gurgle of a little river playing harmony.

Then, in the calm, somewhere unseen, I'd say halfway up a tree, but maybe not, something shrieked. It was a screech of simultaneous surprise and pain. And then a second, weaker screech. In two seconds it was over. Done.

That, I thought, is how animals do it. They prey and are preyed upon. They sneak around in the dark or hide under camouflage. They look for something to eat and try not to get eaten. They eat and get eaten raw.

Nothing ruins the tinkling of ice like a cold reminder about life in the jungle.

Within a second, I thought of my cat. She's a newbie, just off a farm and as yet not definitively named. One name, offered by someone who knows nothing about naming a cat, simply will not work. My tentative moniker, Tiki-Tiki, is really just a clipping of Kitty-Kitty. It doesn't work, either. Because it's a cat. This cat, flat black, invisible in the dark, has not descended far from her feral ancestry. She could live without me. She enjoys the convenience of kibble, but she spends most of her time outdoors enjoying nature.

Had I just heard Tiki-Tiki screech her last? Or had she dispatched some furry little soul to another go-around? Or was it a couple of other forest animals, viscerally instinctive, predestined, anonymous, and, whether prey or preyed upon, doomed to die with a desperate screech?

In any case, the death and the pain of it touched my heart. It's a sad and terrible way for nature to keep itself going, to transfer energy from one beast to another so that yet another and another can have something to eat.

During that brief struggle in the dark, I, a domesticated Deputy Registrar of Voters so far from feral, sat on a deck, tinkling my ice as I recovered from the democratic process.

I couldn't think of a better way for nature to sustain itself, but I appreciated the way we'd just transferred power at the poll. We didn't have to sneak around in the dark. Nobody ate anybody. Nobody screeched with mortal pain. We did what we had to do, and we accept the results. And we'll do it again in November, by which time I'm sure Tiki-Tiki will be home for some civilized chow.

Go Green

What happens after you die?

In one sense, only the dead know.

In another sense, you can have some say in what happens to the body you leave behind.

You can have it sealed up in a heavy-duty, highly varnished, waterproof, rot-resistant, brass-latched box padded on the inside for maximum comfort and encased in a concrete vault, a home-away-from home for the several centuries it will take for your remains to come back to life.

Or you can have 28 gallons of fossil fuel burned to reduce yourself to a sand bereft of anything that would support life, a sand so alkaline that if dumped in a clump under a plant, you'd end up killing it.

Or you can expedite your return to life by being buried naturally: no formaldehyde in your veins, no casket to endure the centuries, no vault to keep the grass above you nice and level for the grim lawnmower.

A burial can be simple: just you in denim and flannel, a shroud of cotton or a casket of plain pine. In no time at all, you join your mother, Earth, and live again.

But you aren't likely to get that simple, natural burial unless you ask for it, and if you're going to ask for it, you'd best do it before the big day. Loved ones are reluctant to opt for the simple, unadorned dispatch. In a gesture of misguided respect, they may try to do everything they can to make your discarded corpse look alive. They will want to give their beloved deceased the best of real estate for eternity. Or they'll opt for cremation, not understanding that sprinkling decarbonized ashes does absolutely nothing for nature.

You can download a Final Request form at ctgreenburialgrounds.org and give your folks a written document they will dare not ignore.

The form lets you specify your disposition, be it green or other. You can name your container, request your cemetery, donate your organs, list your contacts, specify your memorial music and readings, write your epitaph, even request a certain species of tree to be planted over you.

This might take a little research on your part. If you want to go out green, you may have a hard time finding a cemetery that allows it. There aren't many places that will let you become a tree. Connecticut does not yet have a burial ground exclusively for clean, green burials.

If you'd like to make a New Year's resolution that you can easily keep, filling out the Final Wishes Form is a good one. Your time is running out. You'd better do it now.

We Need More Trees

Some of New London's oldest and most prominent residents are under attack. They're being pushed out by cars, stifled by sidewalks, slain by storms, smothered by asphalt, infested with pests, choked by chokers, crippled by senescence and doomed by misnomered development. Since 1993 we've lost a thousand of them.

They continue to die.

"We lost two oak on Prospect St.," says Maggie Redfern, a botanist who cares and keeps track. "One fell over and hit a house. We lost a lot of them on Plant Street, a big sycamore on the corner of Montauk, when they put in new sidewalks. We lost the cherries on Winthrop Boulevard."

Emerald ash borers killed two at Williams Memorial Park. Maggie took me there to see a European beech, a glorious monument of shape and shade. But it was gone. Only a ground-level stump remained, five feet across, powdered with sawdust, still smelling of sawn wood.

We found blonding on some standing ash—pale patches where woodpeckers had tried to hammer in at ash borers under the bark. But the birds won't get them all. The trees are doomed.

Back in about 1850, we lost a buttonwood so towering that its spot on the corner of State and Main (now Eugene O'Neill) is still called Buttonwood Corner. It isn't just a cute name. It's a testament of respect.

Through the course of the 20th century, we lost legions of American elm. They used to lean over streets in leafy arches, shade from sidewalk to sidewalk. In post cards from 1920, the linear forests look like a heaven now long lost. Today we have but three municipal elm—one on Granite, between Williams and Hempstead; another two blocks over, on Broad, a third on Jefferson by Cedar Grove Cemetery.

There are three private-sector elm at the Connecticut College Arboretum, where Maggie is assistant director. But until just recently, there were five. Maggie has some seedlings from the survivors' seed, just possibly resistant to the Dutch elm disease that killed off all the others.

Are these scant survivors resistant or just tolerant of urban stress? Maggie says it's hard to say. Maybe they have escaped the disease because there are so few others to catch it from. The elm used to lean into each other, their branches enlaced like lovers' arms. But they loved too much. They grew too close. They took each other down.

The elm on Granite has it lucky. The city sacrificed some width of street to leave a generous swath of open earth along the sidewalk. Water can seep down to roots, a rare treat for a municipal tree. Long ago, trees along streets and grassy areas beyond them were considered parks. To park one's horse meant to tie it up in the shade. Now we park cars where the parks once were. At best there's a sickly tree in a square yard of earth surrounded by concrete. Its roots buckle the concrete, a futile resistance that dooms it to the chainsaw. A level sidewalk has priority over a living tree.

We lost a lot of trees to the ill conceived urban development of the 1970s–oaks, cherries, pears, katsuras, lindens, crabapples, dogwoods, chokecherries, the sycamore cousins known as London planes, and almost all of the elms that hadn't died by then. We lost three trees all along the quiet street that was made into Governor Winthrop Boulevard. You can see bare squares along the sidewalk just north of the parking garage. There used to be trees there, but nobody remembers what kind. The squares beg replanting, but the owner of the garage says No in fear of branches invading his space.

Who's maintaining the 65 trees planted around the municipal lot on Eugene O'Neill? No one, apparently, so they are slowly choking from the wired collars that helped them grow as saplings.

Maggie and an organization she helped start, New London Trees, have done some planting in the strip down the middle of the boulevard. Two stripling elm are taking a stand at the upper end. Below that, the planters installed three red oak, a good, sturdy, dependable native species that can stand up to hurricanes and asphalt. Below that, some maple and London planes. Why not a well matched monoculture? Well, remember the elms.

Municipal trees may be the biggest bang-for-buck asset that a city can have. They suck up storm water that floods streets, and they grab particulate matter that causes asthma and disease. In New London, each year city's municipal trees inhale over a thousand pounds of carbon monoxide, just as much sulfur dioxide, almost as much nitrogen dioxide, and 21 tons of ozone. They take 3,500 tons of CO_2 from the air and turn it into wood. Over 114,000 tons of CO_2 is stored in city trees. To pull that much CO_2 out of the air by means other than trees would cost over $4 million.

Using trees rather than machines to make these purifications to the air saves New London $171,350 a year, and that number doesn't include other immeasurable financial, aesthetic, health, and psychological benefits. A building surrounded by trees may save 25 percent of its cost of heating and cooling. Trees nurture mental health. Neighborhoods with more trees have less crime. People are willing to trade salary for an office window that looks out on trees. People on leafy streets suffer less stress and live longer. Children are happier around trees.

Despite such benefits, New London has been letting trees die off. According to a detailed inventory orchestrated by Connecticut College student Isabelle Smith, the city had 2,935 municipal trees— that is, trees along streets, in parks, and on school grounds but not in forested areas—in 1993. In 2018, we were down to 1,887.

New London allots about $1,000 to the planting of trees and $1,500 to their maintenance—picayune compared to what the city gets for the investment. Maggie Redfern and New London Trees would like to see that budget increased, and everyone—absolutely everyone—would like to see more trees.

Moby Skunk

One of my favorite neurologists has a skunk problem. At least she says she does. I haven't seen it, but she says it lives under a rock near her swimming pool.

She wants me to trap it, so I will. She scanned my brain once for free. I owe her.

I've trapped her skunks before. I don't know why she has so many. They don't know she's a neurologist. Maybe it's the swimming pool or the little vegetable garden.

I trap them alive, of course. I tempt them with an irresistible delicacy, peanut better on a jaundiced stalk of fridge-wilted celery. They waddle into my trap—a cage-like thing with door at each end—incredulous of their luck, and BAM: their lives are changed forever.

They're never in a good mood when I arrive. They're already putting up a stink so bad it makes my eyes water. I throw a blanket over the trap and hustle it to the back of my pick-up. Then I drive it far away and let it go.

The beast I'm after this time is different. I'm told it's big, fat, and all white. It might not even fit in the trap.

The fear is that it's pregnant. One big, fat skunk today could be five or six skunks around the time the pool opens for the summer.

I'm the kind of twisted individual who would actually enjoy seeing half a dozen big, fat white skunks show up at a pool party. I'm not much of a party person. Definitely more of a skunk person. If skunks showed up at more parties, so would I.

The skunk's notorious defense mechanism is based at two glands located, appropriately enough, on each side of the anus. A powerful muscle can shoot an aromatic outpouring ten feet with a high degree of accuracy.

It's more than a scent. It's a chemical weapon. It can fend off a bear. The human nose can detect it from three miles away. Dogs can smell it from even farther. The difference between bears, people and dogs is that dogs don't care...until it's too late.

It didn't take me long to think of weaponizing a skunk. I know a few people who really need to be put in their place, and nothing brings the haughty down to earth like truth issued from the business end of a Mephitis mephitis.

The neurologist's attorney tells me the Second Amendment doesn't cover weaponized skunks. I feel this is a case for the Supreme Court, but she declines to take on the case.

(She sends this legal counsel from Paris, where, pending an end to the pandemic, she's holed up in a small apartment with her husband and the neurologist's newborn grandson. Skunks are the least of her concerns.)

Connecticut statute Sec. 26-55-6 (3)(B) lumps skunks in with tree kangaroos, African boomslangs, blue-gray gnatcatchers and swamp wallabies, none of which may be imported or possessed in the Nutmeg State. You can get in trouble just for offering succor or comfort to a skunk.

(Parenthetical digression: why do we call it the Nutmeg State when, pound for pound, skunks are by far more preponderant?)

Back to weaponizing. The statute on Category One Wild Animals says nothing about tying a skunk to the handle of someone else's garage door. It does not mention FedEx Same-Day Delivery.

So watch out, ye haughty hypocrites, ye supercilious hoity-toits, ye contemptuous fake-news fans: your life may soon change forever.

Just for the record, you can possess up to six skunks in Arkansas. In Washington, D.C., the limit is one per person. For more information, contact the American Domestic Skunk Association.

The word "skunk" comes from the Algonquian word, "seganku," originating from Proto-Algonquian, "sek-," meaning "urinate," and "akw," meaning "fox."

Fun fact: skunks do not spray other skunks, though in the heat of the mating season, males may hose each other down in hopes of winning their true-love's heart. Fun times!

Skunks are polygynous, meaning that males are willing to mate with more than one female. They do not participate in rearing the young. You may know a skunk or two like that. Please remember that importing or possessing one in Connecticut is illegal. If you must dispose of one, drive it far away and let it go. Which is what we did with Moby Skunk.

The Doom of Wealth

Pope Francis chose the environment as the topic of a major encyclical for a good reason. In the environment – or call it nature – he sees something that knits together the principles and values that are most important to him and his global flock.

The smackdown of nature relates to the suffering of the poor, the worship of money, the wealth gap, the nature of capitalism, the value of families, a world mired in materialism, the discarding of inconvenient people, the threat to life in all its forms. Climate change affects the poor more than the rich. They tend to depend more on nature. Natural disasters hit them harder. They have fewer options when besieged by drought, storm, flood, pollution, or the social unrest that follows radical shifts in the basics of an economy.

Materialism – the pursuit of happiness through things – runs contrary to nature. Every product produced, without exception, requires the destruction of something in nature. Nature can reproduce some of those things, but others cannot grow back.

Under the principles of capitalism, a forest is worth nothing unless cut down. Capital-oriented accountancy has no way to value the oxygen lost, the extinction of species, the warming of distant seas, the far-removed effects on rainfall, the lives of people who depend on the slow, sustainable use of living forest.

The worship of money removes humanity and nature from the center of life. Nature and the dignity of humans are lost in the pursuit of cash. As nature suffers, humankind suffers, especially the poor. The poor become disposable, inconvenient consumers of dwindling resources.

Without much effort, the principle of disposable people extends to foreigners, people of other religions, the elderly, the unborn, the marginal, future generations, and whoever's economies are in conflict with capitalism's need to grow more, consume more, destroy more, discard more.

Pope Francis's encyclical embraces the importance – the miracle – of all life. Many lives and forms of life are threatened by the destruction of the natural environment. The extinction of life on our planet, already taking place, cannot possibly lead to any good. Nature is central to everything. As a moral leader, Pope Francis is obligated to defend nature in the defense of people everywhere. He sees the defense of nature and the prevention of climate change as a moral issue.

How ironic that the head of the Catholic Church is using reason and scientific evidence to counter institutionalized myths based on unprovable claims! How ingenious to base a morality on a global reality.

This encyclical should mark civilization's most significant turning point since the Industrial Revolution. With the industrial production of wealth, society began to turn away from God and the Church, increasingly believing that more physical wealth – more stuff – would bring about happiness.

But something has gone wrong. Physical wealth has not brought spiritual happiness, and the power of commercialism has perverted values to the point where the pursuit of happiness is confused with the pursuit of stuff. We pursue more and more stuff at the expense of nature and disposable people. It looks like progress, but as Pope Francis makes clear, we are moving in the wrong direction.

If we don't turn around, we are going to be very sorry.

Pest or Pal?

I've got a mouse, just a wee thing who lives in the dark of a vent at the back of my stove. I don't know how it got there or what it's like down where it lives. Dark, yes. Dust motes? Skads. Old crumbs? Oh, yeah. Drops of spattered grease? I'm sure.

It's a nice place for a mouse, a mouse from the woods, in for not just the food but the warmth. Why spend five months in the frost when a stove gives you heat, food, nest, and, in a sense, a real home?

All a mouse needs to make a house a home is, yes, kids. Lots of kids. One times ten times five times ten times five.

They add right up. Little mice, first in the nest of motes, then up through the vent to the light and the food left in a pot or pan, that taste of salt, that lick of spice, that grain of rice, that chew of corn to gnaw, that bay leaf that still has a taste of bay.

Yes, I have a mouse like that and, if not now, soon, mice. Times ten.

Then ten times tons.

So I heard her, that mom of tons — rattly-bang, scrape, scuff, clunk — on the steel top of the stove, a mouse in a tiff with a chunk of stale cookie. I went to see, and there I saw, in the slot of the vent, just the snout of a mouse, or half a snout, just the glint of one black-as-night eye, one black bead nose, so small, fixed dead still in fear. And me, too — not in fear as much as doubt.

What to do?

Pound that snout with a...what?...big soup spoon? A slab of steak? A big, fat cook book? My bare fist?

I just stood there, eye to eye, an arm's length from the beast that's been with us since the cave. How could I see fear in a flat-black eye? I don't know, but I saw it. Sensed it. I'm no mouse, but I've been a bit too bold and then too scared to move.

Such a brave mouse, so brave and scared, an inch from her prize and, she knew, what might be her death.

Yes, she. Brave and scared that way, it had to be a she, one with mice to feed, just tots in need of a crumb or two.

Who would move first?

I stood my ground. If she came out, I'd slam the stove or scream hell-to-pay, at least try to scare her back to the woods from whence she came.

I stood for a long time. And then, in a blink, she was gone. There, and then — as if at the same time — not there.

I can't have a mouse in the house. Poop near the food – thoughts of Black Plague – plus it just looks bad.

I went and got a trap – the kind kind, which snaps the neck flat, whack, just like that. No pain, life there and then not there, as if both at the same time, death kissed with the sweet taste of Jif on the tongue. Who doesn't want to go that way? You know how this ends. Of course I couldn't do it. We'd looked at one another too long. We'd grown too close. I felt too much. Or thought too much. I don't know, I guess I'm just a sap. So shoot me.

I stuffed the cookie chunk into the vent and went to bed. There's more than one way to get rid of a mouse. I don't live in a cave. There's no more Black Plague. No rush. I could come up with a plan. I just had to sleep on it. A good dream might do the trick, a nice, deep dream of need and the sweet taste of Jif.

Leave the Leaves Alone

It's that time of year when yellow leaves, or none, or few do hang upon the boughs where late the sweet birds sang. Now all but few are on the ground. My wife and I engage in an annual debate in many ways reminiscent of the Biden-Trump debacle.

At least we're smart enough not to do it on TV.

She wants those leaves disappeared. I want to savor their beauty until it's time to savor the beauty of snow.

The autumn leaves of New England are celebrated. Tourists come from afar to see the surrealism of it all. Media report the wave of color as it eases south. People grapple with the incomprehensibility of it all. They try to photograph the colors—a mountain of it or a single leaf with an impossible blend of orange and green—but such colors cannot be captured.

A sensitive few see beyond the sight of it. Fall comes with its own sweet, musty aroma. It comes with the sound of kids (me among them) scuffing through dry leaves just because they're there. It comes with the utter silence of a leaf departing a twig way up there, just letting go and dancing downward to land without a sound.

Around here, September's a month of blue skies over faint, warm hues of imminent change. October brings rain, pulling down the last of the stragglers and glistening the lollipop colors.

Later, frost edges the leaves with hairs of white. You can't see it from indoors, and it doesn't last long. You have to go outside early and look at it.

On the last day of this September, leaves on the lawn in question reflected the stress of drought. On one side, ruddy leaves of a maple covered the grass. On the other, it was the yellow leaves of a denuded black birch. Many trees around them were still as green as in July.

The deployment of the leaves was like orchestral music in that they told a story without meaning. The crimson leaves were dense around their mother maple but thinned as they stretched across the green and ochre grass. Across the way, the horde of yellow leaves reached reluctantly toward the maple. The grass lay like a valley between them.

I don't know what the scene meant, but it was too perfect to mess with. I let it lie. I watched it as it changed—the leaves browning, blowing around, settling down.

By spring, most will be gone, blown to wherever it is that dead leaves go. They'll be easier to rake in the spring, when it's good to get outside and do something.

There's really no need to mess with leaves now, no need to shriek them away with wind born of an internal combustion engine.

That's what an aesthetically challenged homeowner half a mile away was doing on the last day of September. Yes, I could hear it from half a mile away—his noise scaring *my* leaves on *my* lawn.

Why would anyone want to make so much noise just to blow the beauty from a lawn?

Remember the rake? So quiet, just a swishing whisper of steel tines. As you swished, you could hear birds and crickets. You could converse. You could think and not-think at the same time. It was exercise with a kind of open-air gym equipment, a kind of a back-scratcher for the yard.

One could dispense with the rake, too, by adopting a meadow instead of a lawn. A meadow is a garden that needs no gardener. Its beauty changes through the seasons, opening with dandelions and buttercups in the spring, then Queen Anne's lace and black-eyed Susans all summer, then asters and goldenrod, the harbingers of fall.

I don't know who decided that houses should be surrounded by monochromatic grass. I have a feeling the decision involved money. Keeping a lawn up to snuff requires the purchase of seed, fertilizer, pesticide, poisons, lime, trimmers, mowers, tractors, blowers, gasoline and oil. It requires a lot of noise. It takes a lot of time.

Give me a Monet meadow any day. Give me a Klimt bed of birch leaves. Give me quiet. Give me peace. Give me summer, autumn, winter, spring.

Certain Circles

I can't tell you whom I visited nor where he lives, not even his town. He's not sure if he's legal. He is sure, however, that he wants to stay out of the limelight. He's famous in certain circles, he says, circles in New York, circles that go around the world, circles of art and design. His name is known in Hong Kong. His stuff is worth money.

In his famous days, his money days, he lived on the 35th floor of an apartment on Central Park West. But that was no way to live, people all stacked up on top of each other in little boxes. It wasn't natural. Everything was artificial. Even the flowers in the lobby were artificial. He couldn't live like that.

So in 1981 he walked away from the city, the money, the certain circles, came back to where he grew up, near the high school that taught him art, Norwich Free Academy, Class of '48. He finagled a life-long lease on some land in the woods off a dirt road in a small town where people don't generally care if you've got a clutch of bantams roaming at will, a team of ducks, a muster of peacocks, or rather, now, just four peacocks, the ones too quick for coyotes.

Deer come to him, tempted by the piles of corn he leaves them every day. They know him. When he calls out "It's all right! It's all right!", they come in from the woods. They nuzzle him and eat corn from his hand. They are the most beautiful creatures, he says. So elegant and peaceful. How can hunters kill them? If the hunters want meat, he'll give them hamburger, though he himself does not eat meat. Why all the killing, he asks. Why all the killing? Too many deer? No, he says. Too many people.

He fought in the war in Korea. People tried to kill him. He landed at Inchon, a skin-and-bones kid, tromped over mountains with his M-1, slept in puddles and mud, got crawled on by big fat rats, lived off Red Cross jelly beans, won two medals for valor, another for thirty days straight under enemy fire, came home in one piece, did the New York thing, surrendered, and retreated to Windham County.

He's been building his house for 17 years. He uses second-hand materials, stuff he bums from builders, the remains of demolition. The house looks both ancient and unfinished. It hunkers under low scrub oak, as calm and confident as an English cottage, its steep roof graced with moss, its dormers in four sizes and designs, its old windows blurry with panes of old glass.

It's hard to tell where the woods stop and the yard starts. He likes a house and yard with everything in its place. His house and yard are cluttered with things not yet in their place. He has the things—statues, benches, bird feeders, gnomish odds and ends—and he has the places, but the things are still puzzle pieces waiting to come together. When he's done, 50 or 60 or a hundred years from now, his home will look like a picture on a jigsaw puzzle box.

So far he has no electricity, no running water. He's afraid it might not be legal to live this way. But it's the way he wants to live: out there with nature.

After so many years so close to nature, this is what he's noticed: There are no more birds.

His hand paints the scene with a fluttering sweep. A frenzy of birds used to assault his bird feeder all the time, a chattering free-for-all of titmice, chickadees, cardinals, gold finches, woodpeckers, blue jays and everybody else. His bird feeder is a magnificent homemade edifice with lathed pillars under a shingled roof with a copper weathervane, a Taj Mahal of wild bird eateries.

But now, no birds. Not one. We can't even hear any. He puts a hand to his ear to bring the silence into focus. We listen. We cannot hear a single bird, except...wait...yes, one, in the distance – a crow.

He doesn't like this ominous turn in the way of nature. He suspects the hand of Man. A slight quiver in his clear blue eyes reveals an unspeakable uneasiness with this encroachment of something sneakier than coyotes. He fled Central Park West, but it may have found him. It's out there, and it's not all right, it's not all right.

Here's what worries him more than anything else: That he might die up here in the woods and no one will know that his chickens need feeding, that they might be locked in their coop like so many apartment dwellers trapped on the 35th floor. He thinks some kind of high-tech phone might somehow resolve the problem, but phone lines don't pass anywhere nearby, and cell phone signals haven't found his secret place. Not that he really wants a phone. It just might come in handy that one time.

How Long Can This Hold Out?

A few days ago I savored three thunderstorms that graced the sky over Hanover on a single afternoon. It was sweet–the distant rumble, the uplifting leaves, the darkening horizon, the first drops wafting in on gusts of ozone.

I thought how much people in the Southwest would appreciate such a commonplace Northeast storm. Though summer had yet to arrive, wildfires in California had turned their skies pink and stinky, and Arizona broiled under triple-digit temperatures.

But the lightning of thunderstorms can ignite forest fires. How sad is that? People out west have to both crave and fear rain. It's worse than sad. It's torturous.

Could that happen here, I wondered? Could the regular rains stop, the trees die and dry and burn? Could the streams and brooks trickle down to nothing more than moisture under rocks and memories preserved at historical societies?

I recalled a quatrain from a Shakespeare sonnet:

O how shall summer's honey breath hold out
against the wrackful siege of battering days,
when rocks impregnable are not so stout,
nor gates of steel so strong, but time decays?

Are our rainy days numbered? Could be. A third of the country is under drought conditions this summer. That includes southern Florida and northern Maine, upstate New York and Appalachian Virginia, central Puerto Rico, most of Hawaii, and a vast stretch of Alaska.

Same goes for 85 percent of Mexico. In Canada, Manitoba and Saskatchewan have reached the stage of extreme drought.

Last year, Amazon tributaries were running dry. This year it's record floods. But far south of the Amazon—São Paulo, even Argentina—it's the driest it's been in 111 years.

The Oglala aquifer under the North American breadbasket is dropping by two feet a year, replenishing only three inches. Farmers aren't tapping last year's rainwater. They're tapping paleowater left by glaciers that melted more than 10,000 years ago.

Is New England becoming a literal oasis at the edge of a parched continent? If so, how long can it hold out? How long until America becomes a Sahara from sea to shining sea?

Ever the pessimist, I worry about the collapse of nature—not a total collapse but just enough to reduce the human population to a harmless minimum. Nature can solve its biggest problem with a tactical retreat.

A few years ago, not to be outdone by Shakespeare, I wrote a poem that started off like this:

One of these springs the daffodils
won't melt the snow, the dead snow
will drool into iridescent mud, the fox
won't come around to snatch my hens, no gnats,
no mouse-ear maple buds, no peepers in the dark, the breeze
putrid of whatever they use to embalm Spaghetti-O's...

My poem, like Shakespeare's, ultimately swung around to be about love. His, however, ended with with "...my love may still shine bright," whereas mine saw love wandering "like styrofoam in the desert of the dead."

I'll admit that's a bit melodramatic, but the Bard and I (and Keats, Sandburg, Cummings, Burns, Wordsworth, Tennyson...) sensed a link between love and nature. So I wonder what will be left of love if we're ever deprived of analogies with spring, roses, rain, groves, meadow larks and the honey-breath of summer.

Imagine love and poetry in a post-nature world:

Shall I compare thee to a can of carbonated fructose?
Thou art more lovely and more effervescent.
In you I see grove, rose and warbler oh-so comatose,
and your 401K sings hymns to your sweet investment...

Am I exaggerating or extrapolating? I don't know. I don't even know the difference. But the climactic trajectory does not bode well, and anyone who can't see it isn't looking. New Englanders can still enjoy the pleasures of thunderstorms and brooks, but, well, here comes Shakespeare again:

This thou perceiv'st, which makes thy love more strong,
to love that well which thou must leave ere long.

The Future: All or Nothing?

Ayoung friend recently asked me if today's world is as I had imagined it would be when I was her age.

She meant 45 years ago.

My reflections first tended toward what I didn't see coming–the internet, desktop computers, climate change, gay marriage, a thousand TV channels, or China sending rockets to Mars.

Then I reflected on what I foresaw that never happened: the flying cars, the Hilton on the moon, the humanoid robots, the end of toil, the Age of Aquarius.

Mostly I expected catastrophes. Nuclear war seemed inevitable. The sea would become a lifeless cesspool. Everyone in Africa was going to die of one thing or another. Urbanization would pave the planet and replace nature with a giant machine. Everyone would love some kind of Big Brother. The world would become Hell itself.

The Year 2000 seemed as impossibly distant as 2065 seems now, a time so far that it didn't seem worth worrying about. The new century was when "The Future" would finally arrive. Whatever was to become of civilization, it would happen by the dawn of the new millennium.

How quaint! Now 2000 is the good old days before cell phones, airport security, global quarantines and scorched earth politics.

And here we are, poised about halfway between 1975 and 2045. The technology is amazing but nothing like we expected. The old catastrophes still threaten while new ones seem every bit as bad.

I'm no longer dreaming of flying cars and vacations on other celestial orbs. Star Trek and the Jetson life just aren't going to happen for a long, long time.

And, frankly, I'm having a hard time imagining good things happening.

I can only hope that my fears are as unfounded now as they were when Gerald Ford was president. I was wrong back then; I can only hope I'm still wrong. Maybe nuclear weapons will become obsolete. Maybe the sea won't become a puddle of sludge. Maybe the Big Brother of insidious corporate enticement will consume itself out of existence.

Here's the best that I can hope: As California burns, Miami founders, the midwest dries up, and a plague of virus-infected radioactive locusts descends on the District of Columbia, the reality of climate catastrophe becomes undeniable. The former deniers deny they ever denied.

In a last minute upheaval of public urge, fossil fuels become as shunned as cigarettes and the n-word. No more wars over oil, no spills in the ocean, no carcinogens in the air.

Nature becomes the new god and savior. Nay, not god but goddess. People worship trees. They burn cash in sacrificial ceremonies. Manicured lawns are dismissed as tacky. Neighbors envy each other's front yard meadows and wildflowers.

Time replaces stuff as status. The wealthy brag of how little they own and the naps they take in the afternoon.

A three-day, thirty-hour workweek becomes standard. Month-long vacations are mandatory. Parents have time for children. Citizens have time for democracy. People seek satisfaction not in screen-time but in arts, crafts, cooking, play, education and conversation.

GDPs decline as nations try to strive to produce less as people compete to consume less. Corporations lose their source of power. Consumption of energy spirals down. Renewables suffice.

Calm prevails. Sanity returns. People stop shooting each other. They don't even shout at each other. They have time to think. They agree that hate and anger are bad, peace and understanding good.

But I'm probably wrong. We'll probably be working 80 hours a week to support our labor-saving devices and pay rent for storage of the stuff that won't fit in the garage. The social insanity will worsen. Maybe we'll start a war somewhere, and if that doesn't work, we'll start one somewhere else. We'll tune in to watch forests burn, hurricanes swamp cities and farmers bemoan their cracked earth. We'll watch advertisements tell us we can always have more. We'll change the channel, then change it again and again, a thousand times, searching for something that isn't happening but might.

So Much to See in Flies and Weeds

I've gotten to the point where I'm reluctant to swat a fly. It isn't fear of guilt that stays my hand, nor fear of failure. I know how to do it, I'm pretty good at it, and I've slaughtered flies in my past with a sense of accomplishment and satisfaction.

My success was palpable. Countable. And, yes, justifiable. Synecdochically speaking, flies are airborne bits of excrement and the dead. They pick it up in the great outdoors and bring it to me on their feet, their snouts, their hairy little bellies, their ankles and elbows.

To call these creeps houseflies is like calling Visigoths tourists. I don't think they come in to get out of the heat. They come for the canapés. They head for the kitchen, a veritable smorgasbord after what they were eating in the green, green grass of the back yard.

I've never mourned the passing of a *musca domestica*, not even one of my own. They come to the kitchen asking for trouble. If they've got any fly-sense at all, they know they are taking a big risk to visit the land of milk and honey, pesto, extra virgin olive oil, Fruit Loops, and strawberries flown in from—I swear I'm not making this up–Chile. If they're any kind of fly at all, they know they're in the realm of Raid and swatters.

Not that I would spray chemicals anywhere around my Fruit Loops. I'd sooner have a flock of flies with dirty feet and fecal grins. But I have a swatter and I'm not afraid to use it. It's nothing special, just a cheapy with a coat-hanger handle and deadly woven mesh made in, bless it, Honduras.

I was in Honduras once, and believe me, they know about flies. They had–and this is going back a few decades–a lot of swatting to do. I'm sure somebody regrets sending my swatter to the Gales Ferry Ocean State Job Lot. Some wife on the outskirts of Tegucigalpa is probably swatting her husband with a dish towel and screaming, "You sent it WHERE?"

But I digress. I was going to confess my feelings of guilt over even the slightest injury against nature, even anything as seemingly insignificant as wasting a fly.

Insignificant? It's hard to say. Here's what poet Ogden Nash had to say about it:

"God in His Wisdom made the fly

And then forgot to tell us why."

Actually flies work a key niche in nature, but it's too disgusting to describe here, so I'll just segue to another pest I'm learning to leave alone, namely, weeds–the photosynthetic equivalent of a fly.

I've been reading about the impending doom of civilized life, if not human life, as the atmosphere heats up and most people's reaction is limited to cranking up the a/c and flopping down on the couch to deny reality over a cold beer and a bucket of extra-strength Doritos.

In each fly I see a reminder of the ephemerality of life. In weeds I see a sprout of hope. Much though I love the royal redwoods and the open-armed majesty of our local sycamores, I suspect our salvation may be in the dandelions, the goldenrod, even the bittersweet and poison ivy. They are the survivors that defy all attempts to swat them from our lawns and gardens. They just might be our saviors, our last hope as the seas rise, the forests burn, and the breadbasket turns to dust and blows away. Weeds might even be our last meal and the source of our last breaths of oxygen. They might even be our survivors, and I wouldn't blame them if they look as smug as a fly in butter when we're gone.

Big Ideas and Questionable Intents

Dog Be with You

Mandatory dog accompaniment may be the best idea since unsliced bread and cross-country golf. Granted, that latter invention hasn't received the attention it deserves, but the dog idea is one whose time has come.

MDA is the legal requirement that all people be accompanied by a dog wherever they go. If two people walk down the street, they need two dogs. If a dozen slackers are hanging out at the Dutch Tavern, there are 13 dogs there—twelve for the customers, plus one to maintain order while her companion human tends bar.

Picture it: Dogs horsing around school playgrounds. Dogs sniffing people at City Hall. Dogs keeping people's feet warm at the Garde. Dogs getting seasick on the Block Island Ferry. It's going to be so much fun!

Consider the impact on crime. Nobody mugs somebody who's with a dog. Burglars don't sneak into homes that have dogs. Dogs can smell gunpowder and drugs. And who's going to rob a bank if it's going to involve a lot of barking?

Dogs are good for business, the foundation of an entire industry—dog food, dog accessories, dog training, dog walking, dog grooming, dog shows and, with so many dogs in town, dog accommodations.

In other words, dogs can be jobs, products, services, and money. Isn't that what everybody wants?

But it isn't just the economy. Dogs are pals. They're family. They're loved. A new puppy is of interest to the whole neighborhood. The death of a dog makes people cry. There's something about a dog that brings out the human in us, which is really something to think about.

And in a nation torn by cultural and political strife, I think we can all agree that we don't need to ask the dogs about MDA. They don't care! Unlike cats, gerbils and goldfish, they're always up for adventure, even if it's just a walk on a leash. And they're going to go nuts over restaurants!

Speaking of which, any restaurant worth its salt is going to expand its menu to include a little dog food. And if I know Americans—and I've known quite a few, some of them real doozies—they aren't going to be comfortable letting their best friends be served some kind of crap out of a can. Who's going to a restaurant that doesn't have a bone or two among the specials of the day?

And yes, you'll need to take your mandatory companion when you go to the rest room. Of course. But don't worry about his or her gender. As I said, they don't care! And if a human of questionable or objectionable gender walks in, it isn't going to be a problem. Who's going to get weird in a rest room full of dogs?

If you call an ambulance, you know what's going to happen. Two EMTs, a paramedic and three dogs will jump out the back. This will be not only thrilling to watch, but medically beneficial as well. Dog spit is bactericidal.

In ancient Greece, dogs were trained to lick wounds. In around 1320, St. Roch was cured of plague after his dog licked his festering buboes. In 1970, the medical journal "Lancet" published an article, "Dog Licks Man," that reported dog saliva healing a wound.

As they say in France, "Langue de chien, langue de médecin." (A dog's tongue is a doctor's tongue.)

(On the other hand, it depends on what was last in Dr. Dog's mouth. It probably wasn't Listerine. Dog licks have resulted in sepsis, necrosis, spinal infections, meningitis, and in rare cases, rabies. Other side effects may occur. Ask your doctor if dog spit is right for you.)

Let's face it: dogs deserve to be with us. They were our first domesticated animals. Over the course of 15,000 years, they've adapted to our behavior. They're adapted to the point where they couldn't live without us. (As opposed to cats, most of whom are just a few generations away from feral. They'd be fine on their own. They might like us, but they don't need us.)

All it takes to make MDA a reality in Connecticut is a single vote by the General Assembly. Write to your state reps and senators today and tell them what you think!

What This County Needs: Tough Golf

Tough golf: it's the game we need in today's world.

The rules are no different from those of the old-fashioned game that has outlived its environmental appropriateness. The difference is in the course. Tough golf takes the golfer into the woods, over mountains, down canyons, through thickets, and into territory new not just topographically but environmentally, economically, and psychologically.

It's not a game for the wimps and wusses who expect a buzzcut carpet of bentgrass, no obstacle less benign than a shallow pond or sculpted sand trap. It's a game for the hearty and robust, the free and the brave, the frontiersperson all Americans imagine themselves to be.

As such, tough golf is reminiscent of the Westward Movement away from the restrictions of urban life and into the challenges of the new and unknown. For that reason, the proper tough golf game is always played east to west, that most American of directions, the one toward independence, prosperity, and a new future.

The tough golf course is simple and low-budget—just holes in the woods and discreet flags to mark them. The fancier courses might offer a rudimentary map. Trespassing may be part of the game. So are balls ricocheting off trees.

Not part of the game: clearing brush, trimming branches, sweeping leaves, smoothing earth, whining about the weather or making a lot of noise. Leaving a ball behind forfeits the game.

It's what America needs—a bipartisan sport that can be enjoyed by tree-huggers and Trumpistas alike. It lets players invade nature while preserving it as a kind of obstacle course that photosynthesizes.

As such, the tough golf course is a perfect fit for today's environmental concerns. It does not require replacing 50 acres of forest or field with a lawn that needs fertilizer, pesticides, water and mowers. The course itself provides shade, topsoil, birdsong, uplifting breezes, and plenty of places to sit.

The tough golf course requires minimal maintenance and expenditure. It just needs to be preserved for its natural beauty and random challenges. Nothing gets modified, which is to say messed up, for the golfer's convenience. Swamps, thorns and boulders are metaphors for much of life. The tough golfer deals with them.

If you search the Internet for "golf challenge," you will get 148 million hits. But not one explains what's so challenging about crossing a fairway in stretchy chinos or a pastel skirt. Not one of them mentions such real and rigorous challenges as copperheads, poison ivy, bears, swamp muck, mosquitos, deer ticks, deer hunters, cliffs, sleet, map-reading, magnetic north, or the weight of ammunition.

I'll tell you the challenge I'd like to see: one of America's hotshot golfers smacking a ball through grizzly territory for 48 hours without benefit of cart or caddy. I can think of one semi-pro in particular, recently unemployed, overweight, and without much else to do. Golf like that I could watch on TV—the ultimate reality show!

Yes, 48 hours. Why not? Or 48 days. Or more. Theoretically, one could spend a month golfing Yosemite, which my attorney tells me would be perfectly legal. I can imagine a tough golf iditarod— iditagolf!—up the Appalachian Trail. A really serious golfer could sink thousands of holes between Caribou and San Diego or, for that matter, Patagonia. What would it take? Just time and lots of holes.

Or, in a variation, just one hole far, far away. It's more like a marathon. No need to count strokes. First golfer to get there wins.

Tough golf's predecessor is an existing game called cross-country golf, a hybrid of the even wussier traditional game. A golfer tees off at, say, the second hole of a golf course but drives as directly as possible toward the fifteenth hole, even if it means clearing a wooded area. The next leg heads straight over to the ninth hole, and then over a hill to the twelfth. Golfers get their adventure and smooth putting greens.

Southeastern Connecticut is perfect for tough golf. Plenty of woods. A challenging topography. Not many bears. A population of Yankees with a genetic tendency toward independence and tightfistedness. Its time we shed our stupid Nutmeg moniker and be known as the Land of Tough Golfers.

Does New London Need a Back-Up Mascot?

Sports fans and the political cognoscenti are well aware of the controversy rending the town of Killingly. From 1939 until 2019, the Killingly High School teams were known as the Redmen. But last year, under pressure from several Native American tribes, the school board voted to adopt a new mascot, the Red Hawks.

Students and faculty generally accepted the change, but voters did not. Republicans running for the school board vowed to rescue the historical mascot. In November, the party took the majority on the board. This January, in a contentious five-hour meeting, the board rescinded the new name and mandated the return of the Redmen.

This is America, so the issue is probably not resolved. For one thing, no one has opined on whether female teams should be called the Redwomen. For another, there's talk in Hartford of a bill to prohibit certain categories of team names. And that's where New London comes in.

New London High School has a respectable mascot: the Whaler. It reflects the historical foundation of the city's glorious past, and it acknowledges the courage and fortitude of those who sailed the seas when ships were made of wood and men were made of steel and nothing was made of plastic. And if there were any female whalers, they are included in that delightfully gender-neutral term.

So everybody should be happy, right?

Well, not necessarily, for, as stated above, this is America. Sooner or later someone's going to pipe up about the poor whales. Do the high school teams want to be known as the type to skewer their fellow mammals for their oil and spermaceti?

We don't need to answer that question quite yet. But it wouldn't hurt to have a back-up mascot—one that inflicts fear on its opponents yet reflects today's sensitivities.

The Nutmeg state's usual perpetrators of ferocity—sharks, bears, wolves, rattlesnakes, falcons, eagles, wildcats, pirates, or, for that matter, red hawks and whalers—just aren't cutting it these days. Their death tolls don't even reach the single digits. Opposing teams just don't take them seriously anymore.

It's tempting to enlist the second-most dangerous animal in Connecticut—the featherless biped. They've been running rampant across the state, wrecking cars, felling forests, casting their waste into the public air supply, making horrific noises in the night, breeding willy-nilly, mating in parking lots and elevators, and electing Republicans to boards of education.

But featherless bipeds are also a sensitive bunch, and not without reason. They have personal flaws, phobias, foibles, funny bones, faint hearts, fallibilities, fecklessness, foot fungus, fetiches, finicalities, foolhardiness, fusspottedness, futilitarianism, pathological frugality, philosophical tendencies, and just about every other F-word in the dictionary other than feathers.

In other words, we'd best just leave them alone.

But there's a more ferocious animal that is very much indigenous to our state. Everyone fears it, and innumerable Nutmeggers have been attacked by it. They are especially rampant on the southeast coast where whalers once roamed. They cause a gasp of horror whenever they are found. No team wants to trot out onto a field to face them.

Yes, that ferocious, native American beast is that tiny-weeny bloodsucker *Ixodes ricinus*, known among the cognoscenti as the deer tick. I'm not suggesting that the New London Deer Ticks is necessarily the best team name, but maybe we should snag it while it's still available.

On Red

Norwich Arts Center has announced the theme of its February gallery show. It will be the color of passion, heat, burgundy, roses, rubies, lips, love, and the seat of love, the target of Cupid's bow, the heart.

Yes, the theme is red.

Red's been expressing since prehistoric times. It was mankind's first pigment. It's the Paleolithic smears of red ochre clay on the walls of Lascaux in France, Serra da Capivara in Brazil, Pinnacle Point in South Africa, Zhoukoudian in China, and Leang Tedongnge in Indonesia.

Women of ancient Egypt used red ochre to put blush on their cheeks, flare in their hair, and passion on their lips.

Titian, Bruegel and Vermeer used the red root of the madder plant for brilliant vermilions. The Aztecs squished cochineal insects to make scarlet for headdresses. Ancient Greeks dried female Kermes to make a crimson dye. Brazil got named after a reddish wood that looked like "brasas" — embers — and which produced a reddish dye prized by European royalty.

Red: the icon of love and blood, blush and hot lips, passion and aggression, anger and war, communists and Republicans, Trump ties, stop signs and sunsets, sex and the devil and God's wounds. It's more than a color. It's a symbol.

Symbolic red goes beyond its end-of-the-rainbow wave. It *means*. You can roll out a red carpet without having an actual carpet. You can raise a red flag without a flag, be broke without red ink, cut red tape without scissors, paint a town red without paint, and catch someone red-handed in a red-light district on a red-letter day even if it's dark.

In February, red means Valentine's Day. It's the color of the blood-flushed heart. It's the cheek-pink of one suffering from idiopathic craniofacial erythema.

It's the hue of the amethyst St. Valentine himself (one of several, actually, and no one knows which) supposedly wore in a ring engraved with an image of the putto Cupid.

Though the several St. Valentines were all known as nice guys — one of them surreptitiously officiated forbidden weddings for Roman soldiers — they weren't associated with romance until 1382, when Chaucer wrote about parliamentary birds choosing mates on St. Valentine's Day. For St. Valentine of Rome, that would be February 14.

A few centuries later, the date became an opportunity (or obligation) to express romantic love. In 1797, a British publisher issued "The Young Man's Valentine Writer" for dudes desperate for a sentimental quip. It wasn't until 1784 that a book of nursery rhymes established our most adaptable couplet, plus a little more:

> The rose is red, the violet's blue,
> The honey's sweet, and so are you.
> Thou art my love, and I am thine:
>
> I drew thee to my Valentine:
> The lot was cast and then I drew,
> And Fortune said it shou'd be you.

February 14 is an annual opportunity to get a certain something done. You know what it is. But do you know what works to make it happen?

Wine works. Chocolate works. A candle-lit dinner works. But nothing works like a work of art, the gift most likely to be consumed forever.

The NAC Gallery at 62 Broadway offers art aimed at the heart. Some of it goes for the price of chocolate. Some of it's around the price of a meal at a fine restaurant that's probably closed.

NAC isn't closed on Saturdays in February, noon to four. Red isn't the only color. There are others. They are all good, and they work.

Just for Hics and Giggles

Once upon a time, there were a little girl named Gaby and a big boy named Barack. Gaby was in the eighth grade while Barack was being inaugurated president. It was an inconvenient time for either to get hiccups.

Unfortunately, it was Gaby who got them. She was watching the inauguration on TV at school. She hicked, and then she giggled, and the giggle made her hic. As she spiraled into constitutional disrespect, Mr. Marsico dispatched her to the principal's office. Hicking and giggling down the hall, she was a little scared but also relieved to get out of class. In such times, hiccups are good.

Gaby got off easy. Not only was she not given detention or charged with something akin to sedition, but her hiccups went away in a matter of minutes. Doctors never discovered the cause of her affliction. In fact, they didn't even try.

But the causes could have been any of many, including a hair touching the eardrum, a cyst on the neck, a tumor in the brain, a tumor somewhere else, devious elves, gastrointestinal reflux, laryngitis, encephalitis, meningitis, pneumonia, multiple sclerosis, stroke, traumatic brain injury, alcoholism, anesthesia, barbiturates, diabetes, electrolyte imbalance, kidney disease, chemotherapy, spicy food, carbonated beverage, steroids, opioids, malfunctioning pacemaker, or weighing a hog.

Actually, there's been only one confirmed case of someone coming down with hiccups while weighing a hog. This was in 1922, when it was delightfully normal for a man to be lifting up 350 pounds of unprocessed pork.

But something went wrong. The man, Charles Osborne, fell, pig in hand, banging his head on the way down and breaking a tiny blood vessel in his brain. He didn't feel a thing, but the hog was executed, hung on a hook, cut into pieces and eaten by scores of American consumers.

Osborne wasn't so lucky. As soon as he hit his head, he began to hiccup 40 times per minute. This went on for years. His wife divorced him, but he married a second, who didn't seem to mind. They had eight children.

Over the years, he managed to slow his hics to 20 per minute, but it was still hard to eat. He had to blend his food into a liquid to be able to swallow during brief opportunities.

It is estimated that Osborne hiccuped 438 million times in 68 years. Then one day he simply stopped. A year later, he died. He was 97.

Jennifer Mee, known to American consumers as the "Hiccup Girl," was about Gaby's age in 2007, when she came down with a case of synchronous diaphragmatic flutter so bad she hicked 50 times a minute for 35 days, long enough for her to appear on various TV shows and become a national celebrity.

Later that year, after the hiccups stopped, she ran away from home. Three years later she was arrested for involvement in a vicious robbery in which a victim was shot four times with a .38. Jennifer pleaded sort-of innocent. Her lawyer sort-of blamed Tourette's syndrome for the hiccups and the murder. A jury found her plenty guilty of the latter and sentenced her to life in prison without parole.

It wasn't her fault. She'd tried breathing into a paper bag, standing on her head, bending way over and drinking water, eating a big wad of peanut butter, and putting sugar under her tongue. Also, she didn't actually pull the trigger.

Other cures: Salt in yogurt. Cardamom tea. Chew ginger. Hold your breath. Hold a pencil in your teeth and drink a glass of ice water. Try again with warm water. Get scared. Sing loudly. Laugh loudly. Breathe carefully, thoughtfully.

Check your genetics. Hiccups go way back. Amphibians were the first hiccupers. It was a way to pull oxygen through their gills. In time, they grew lungs, kind of like the way gilled tadpoles turn into pulmonary frogs.

One thing led to another, and now all mammals hiccup. Dogs. Bears. Bats. Whales. A fetus hiccups in the womb, even without air to hic. It's an underwater myoclonic jerk of the diaphragm, a trial run at actual breathing. It could be said that one's first breath is a hiccup.

But back to Gaby: It would be fortunate indeed if we had a president inaugurated while he or she had the hiccups. Imagine it... "I do solemnly (hic) swear that I will faithfully (hic) execute..." And then he or she giggles, and then hics again. That's what we need. In such times, hiccups are good.

On Chocolate

Where were you on July 7? It was World Chocolate Day! If you weren't wolfing down a few pounds of the stuff, you were negligent. The chocolate cops are going to come after you.

But not to worry. Milk Chocolate Day is coming up on July 28. There's an International Chocolate Day on September 13, and if you miss that, there's White Chocolate Day on September 22, and National Chocolate Day on October 28 and yet another NCD on December 28, just a couple weeks after National Cover Anything in Chocolate Day, December 16, on which date all businesses and government offices will be closed so that people can stay home and do what needs to be done.

We have chocolate today thanks to the Mayans, who were enjoying xocolatl for 34 centuries before Christopher Columbus discovered it on his fourth voyage to India. (Lest history judge him wrong, let it be known that when he came across several local people paddling a canoe full of cocoa, he stole their precious crop.)

The Mayans consumed xocolatl as a hot beverage. The Aztecs imported it and drank it cold, or at least as cold as it gets in Mexico. They called the drink cacahuatl, literally "cacao water."

Both peoples associated cacahuatl with human sacrifice because the brew looked like blood. The Spanish thought it looked like something else, so for marketing purposes, they dumped the "caca-" and opted for a brand name more like xocolatl.

But don't let such facts ruin your Cover Anything in Chocolate Day.

(Etymological pause: caca dates back to the Proto-Indo-European ancestor of several modern languages. Derivatives of caca appear in Spanish, Greek, Russian, Hebrew, Gaelic, Finnish, Turkish, Icelandic, and Persian (but not Aztec), always referring to you-know-what. Our "poppiecock" comes from a Dutch word, pappe kak, meaning "diarrhea." Derivatives also pop up in cacophony (bad sound), coprophagy (bad job) and kakistocracy (bad government.)

As long as we're on words, let's clarify something you've always wondered: cocoa is the fruit of the cacao tree.

We know where caca, cocoa and cacao come from, but we have no idea where National Cover Anything in Chocolate Day comes from other than the obvious fact that she was an absolute genius.

While the plethora of chocolate-based holidays seem to have the year well covered, there are still opportunities for a place like New London as it struggles to make a name for itself.

There is no Chocolate Capital anywhere.

There is no Chocolate Hall of Fame.

There is no statue dedicated to Chocolate.

There is no statue made of Chocolate.

There is no statue that has been dipped in Chocolate.

There is no official celebration of Cover Anything in Chocolate Day.

So here's a question: How much of this confectionary vacuum could a city like, say, New London fill?

As New London struggles to draw the world's attention—and ideally some of its money, too—maybe chocolate is the key, the Punxsutawney Phil that puts the city on the media map.

So here's the plan: Every National Cover Anything in Chocolate Day, with all due pomp and ceremony, the city should dip its toppled statue of Christopher Columbus in a vat of bubbling dark chocolate. What better way to honor the first European to steal cocoa beans?

Such an event would certainly garner as much media attention as a groundhog. The world is nuts about chocolate. Global annual sales are $83 billion, half of it in Europe. The United States consumes only 18 percent of it. The British each eat an average of 24 pounds of it each year, about as much seafood as they eat. Americans, paragons of temperance, eat only half that much.

A few West African countries produce 60 percent of the world's cocoa, but the entire African continent consumes only 3.28 percent of the world's chocolate.

And that brings us to the dark side to chocolate. Though the world loves the stuff, cocoa farmers in Ivory Coast, which produces more than any other nation, earn less than a third of the U.N. poverty level of $2 a day. In that country and Ghana, 2.1 million children work in cocoa fields, and an estimated 12,000 of them in Ivory Coast are slaves subjected to harsh and abusive conditions.

Governments and chocolate companies have vowed to do something about the situation, but according to The Cocoa Barometer, "Not a single company or government is anywhere near reaching their commitments of a 70 percent reduction of child labour by 2020."

Maybe dipping a statue in boiling chocolate will give certain kakistocratic government and corporate authorities something to think about.

Following the Words

I'm almost done translating a classic Brazilian children's novel by Monteiro Lobato. There's just one little problem: its racism.

Among the many things the world doesn't need right now, along with nuclear war, deadly pandemics, and collision with an asteroid, is a racist children's book.

But that's what I've got. That's what I've been working on for months. Now the question is what to do with it.

If the book–my translated title is *The Fancies of Littlenose*–had been written in the past few decades, I'd neither translate it nor even read it. I'd relegate it to the rubbish. I'd bury it in leftovers. I wouldn't even dignify it with recycling.

If I could edit the original, I could easily excise the offensive references and still have an entertaining and imaginative piece of fantasy literature.

But the original was published in 1931, and who am I to edit a classic?

It isn't a terrible or hateful racism, but it's certainly disrespectful. The story involves one Black person. She is a servant to a white person. She is referred to as a "negra" more often than by her name. She is loved by the other characters, but once the narrator refers to her by a term that could mean either "esteemed negra" or "pet negra"—both offensive yet at the same time meant to be affectionate.

(Astute readers are now wondering why an upper-case B in Black but a lower-case w in white. The New York Times recently decided to do it that way, and I think their reasoning is reasonable. I'll let you look that up so I can move on.)

Having been written in the early 20th century in a country still recovering from slavery, the book reflects the racism that our own country still wrestles with.

So what to do with it?

Edit out the offensive part so we can pretend the racist attitude never happened? That seems a lot like erasing history by editing it.

Or simply not translate it? That seems a lot like trying to erase history by ignoring it, tantamount to burning a book or tearing down a statue.

We've faced these questions before with *Huckleberry Finn*, a book considered fundamental to American culture. It is replete with racism and integral to the American soul. It's about the way we were: racist to an extreme yet bold enough to seek to escape it.

The main issue with that book is the word used to describe Huck's friend Jim, a word so ugly we avoid repeating it even in an academic discussion. At least one modern edition rewords the epithet as "the slave Jim."

But now "slave" is considered offensive, implying that a slave is inherently someone's property. The preferred term is "enslaved person."

I can't argue with the good intentions of that shift in correctness, but I feel the American soul loses something if Huck Finn decides to go to Hell for stealing "formerly enslaved person Jim." Something terribly important and too terrible to forget gets lost in that translation.

The Fancies of LittleNose depicts racist attitudes of the past—not just Brazil's but America's. It also depicts the past of anyone who has experienced childhood, with all its fantasies and whimsy.

Cultures have fantasies, too. Racism is one of them. It's a fantasy based on imaginary characteristics associated with millions of strangers. Racists believe in their fantasies much the way children believe in Santa Claus and tooth fairies.

We cannot abhor racism unless we know about it. To ignore it, cover it up, erase references, or forget that it ever existed does not do away with it. History happened. It's where we were. Toppling statues and burning books is a counterproductive way to avoid repeating it.

I'm going to finish my translation as faithfully to the the original as possible. But I'm going to take the chicken way out. I'm going to discuss the racism (and also a little sexism) in an Introduction, and I'll tag a few references with footnotes. Readers shouldn't need that, but they're going to get it anyway. I hope they're not offended by my gratuitous excuses.

And I'm not going to have the book illustrated. I don't want children to read it. Not until they're older. Not until they, unlike racists, can think beyond fantasy.

Ideas: So Precious and Ephemeral

I had an idea the other day. It popped up from the place all new ideas pop from—nowhere. For billions of years there was no idea, and then the idea came into its little non-thing existence, and then...

...and then it was gone, blipped back into the darkness like some kind of muon from the great beyond.

It was a great idea. I sensed its grandness in its microseconds of glory. But I remember nothing else about it, not even a little. I have a lingering image of a Flexible Flyer but also of a caloric comparison of one bowl of cookie dough ice cream and three bales of Shredded Wheat. It might have had something to do with literacy in Kenya. Whatever it was, it would have solved a big chunk of civilization's problems. But just like that...pffft...it's gone.

I mourn the loss. A good idea is more precious than a diamond. (Never mind the bad ideas. I've had plenty of them, too.) Psychologists and philosophers have long looked for the source of ideas. Best they can figure is that ideas come from somewhere in the head, but no one knows how they get in there. For all anybody really knows, they're from the elbow.

Abraham Loeb, chair of the astronomy department at Harvard, wrote in Scientific American, "Ideas originate from pregnant minds, just as babies emerge from the bellies of their mothers."

He then went on to ask, "What makes a mind fertile?"

His brief answer: "The freedom to venture without the confines of traditional thinking or the burden of practical concerns."

That said, Loeb lists a few contraceptives that can help prevent the birth of an idea. One is to have the free drift of thoughts interrupted. Another is to be immersed in the trivia of common wisdom. Another is to live in an echo chamber of ideas similar to your own. Another is the readiness of others to declare an idea stupid because it hasn't been pre-approved.

Culture (traditional thinking) and economics (practical concerns) do what they can to suppress ideas, but ideas happen nonetheless. Culture may be the baggage of the past, but it's baggage that's ready to hop on a train to someplace new. Likewise, practical concerns, such as feeding oneself, may burden the mind with toil, chores, and the necessary. But necessity gives birth to innovation.

In other words, civilization never stands still for long and is always in conflict between the tried-and-true and the daring-and-new. Defenders of the former deny the failures of the past while fearing the probable failures of new ideas. Defenders of the latter are too young, dumb, or optimistic to know that the truly innovative will indeed probably fail.

But sometimes it doesn't. Despite the alarms of conservatives, the deafening echoes of antiquated certainties, and the dazzling distractions of the latest gewgaws, an idea sprouts and takes root in a fertile mind.

My ideas come along when I can least do anything with them. In the shower. Driving a car. Listening to crickets in the dark. Listening to peepers at a party. All of a sudden a mental bell goes "Ding!" A light comes on. A pathway through the 21st century is illuminated with the clarity of the perfectly obvious. Eureka! I found it!

And then, for lack of a pencil, I lose it.

I know what you're thinking: carry a pencil, stupid. But I know from experience that a pencil in the pocket somehow wards off ideas.

There's something to be said for boredom—those increasingly rare moments when we're free from screens, entertainment, conversation, or the need to focus—those precious, spaced-out moments when you're not even seeing what's right in front of you. Your mind wanders through a foggy, pathless forest until an idea steps out from behind a tree like a little leprechaun with a twinkle in his eye.

And then you think: Are all leprechauns male? And how come you never see two of them together? Are they anti-social or do they just not trust each other? Do they hanker for a pal? Maybe they need a place where they can get together for a drink...a bar for lonely leprechauns! Now there's an idea...

Webs We Weave

Lying. We all do it, and it's done to us all.

We have a lot of words for it: Fibs. Shams. Whoppers. Yarns. Red herrings. Myths. Fairy tales. Propaganda. Trumped-up terminological inexactitude.

There are bald-based and bold-faced lies, white lies and blue lies. We bluff. We puff up and cover up. We deceive, defame, and disinform. We weasel and wax ironic. We fake, falsify, fabricate, prevaricate, confabulate, defraud and dissimulate. We speak with forked tongue in cheek. We con, twist, omit, and spin. We pile it on. We call it bull, B.S. and baloney and shovel it into crocks.

I know one such crock. It calls itself Country Crock. It isn't a crock. It's a plastic tub of congealed vegetable oil from the friendly farmers at Unilever. The fake crock bears a picture of a nonexistent barn on a fake and frilly placard faked with woodgrain. Above, it says, "Shedd's Spread," but Shedd does not exist. Below, a fake scroll says, "Country Fresh Taste."

I live in the county. Its fresh tastes are many: pine sap, pond water, sassafras, honey, mint, wild garlic, trout, raspberries, with aromas of rain, skunk, manure, and mown hay. But fresh congealed vegetable oil? Never.

Advertisers lie to buyers. Robots call us up to lie. Spin doctors blur lies into a foggy notion of maybe.

And that's not all.

We lie to ourselves. ("This isn't happening.")

We lie to simplify. ("Fine, whatever.")

We lie in politeness. ("How interesting!")

We lie in the name of love. ("Of course I love you!")

We lie to kids to give them hope. (Everything's going to be all right, and Santa Claus is coming to town!)

Men dress in pinstripe lies and lie about how much sex they've had. Women paste their lips with lies and lie about how little sex they've had.

Good fiction is a good lie, and it's even better if the lie tells the truth.

We live at the end of pipelines of lies. They're on TV. They're on the internet. They come in the mail and over the phone. They're dressed in the folderol of ads, packaging, junk mail, lawn signs, memes, sermons, soundbites, biases, platitudes, stereotypes. We usually know they're lies. And the liars know we know they're lying.

But without lies, what's left? Sometimes they're all that hold us together. No less than Napoleon said, "History is a set of lies agreed upon."

Candidates try to pull us together with cherry-picked half-truths in the guise of patriotism, accusation and hope. We know they're lies, so we vote for the liars whose lies we like, the lies that bespeak the way we wish life was. We hope the lies are gift-wrapped packages containing kernels of truth. And sometimes they are.

Lies come in so many packages and with so many intents and varying values that we have a taxonomy for them. To name a few...

The noble lie, told for the greater good but not without benefit to the liar.

The honest lie, really just a mistake without intent to deceive.

The white lie, harmless, told when the truth would hurt.

The blue lie, told by police to ensure conviction of the accused.

The big lie, so audacious that it seems beyond the scope of credibility.

The bluff, a tactic to gain advantage.

The defamatory lie, targeted on harming a reputation.

The half-truth lie, especially effective because it uses a fact to deceive.

The trade lie, a natural part of advertising, public relations, sales, politics, and other sad professions.

The jocular lie, the truth in an untrue jest, the tall tale, the deception of irony.

The fantasy lie, sometimes shared, sometimes kept to ourselves, in either case functional only if credible.

The lie of silence, the implied acceptance of a lie as truth.

We all live lies, like lies, need lies, and deal with lies. But lies are trouble. They require a commitment of memory and imagination. They are an indulgence that leads to suffering. Once revealed, they call all subsequent truth to question.

And they eventually fall apart. You can fool some of the people some of the time, and facts can be denied, but not for long. Tangled webs unweave. Truth necessarily prevails.

The only question is, does it prevail in time?

Uncertain Times

The Fiery Cauldron of Necessity

I got a bit upset by the impeachment thing. Who didn't? The process was ugly, the result disturbing, the implications chilling. I didn't quite see the demise of democracy, but I could hear it rumbling just over the horizon.

I wasn't the only one worried. In a sad sense, Americans had reached a consensus. Everyone agreed that we had a problem. We just didn't agree on what the problem was. Was it okay for a president to use foreign aid to induce another country to get involved in our election? Was it okay for Congress to investigate the executive branch? Did the president really need to comply with every subpoena that came along? To what extent might a president disobey laws? Can any presidential candidate use taxpayer dollars to get political help from a foreign government, or is that a privilege only for an incumbent? Can other candidates ignore subpoenas?

I wanted a solution. And solace. Surely some kind of legislation could clarify the Constitution, reiterate the responsibility of

Congress, and draw a bright line around presidential obligations and authority.

So I looked for someone who knows law, studies history, and has actually served in public office. U.S. Representative Joe Courtney fit the bill, but he was, to say the least, busy. So I went with New London's own Daryl Finizio, former mayor and current attorney who happens to be working on a book about the frailties and historical foundations of the Constitution.

Attorney Finizio did not cheer me up. He said, "Roosevelt told the greatest generation that they had a rendezvous with destiny. I believe the younger generation of today has a rendezvous with revolution."

Dang! Sorry I asked! But it was too late to seek out cheerier prognostication. We were sitting in his office, a parlor in his house with a desk no larger than necessary and a wall hung with more than enough diplomas.

No, he told me, legislation will not work. Neither will court decisions. The Constitution is very clear about Congressional oversight over the executive branch. It's clear that the president and cabinet secretaries must answer to Congress. They cannot ignore a subpoena. They are not above the law. If they are investigated and accused by Congress, they must answer for it. And Congress cannot take No for an answer.

The only remedy for crimes and misbehavior by the president, Mr. Finizio said, is impeachment and removal from office. Congress failed in that oversight obligation, and in so doing, it opened the legal floodgates to that kind of activity in government. The president has tacit approval to use foreign aid for his personal benefit. The president can ignore subpoenas and investigations. The president has transcended the Constitution.

"The Constitution is clear," Finizio said, "and if it failed to control the president, then it failed. A law on top of that won't help."

The solution, he said, "Sounds nuts...until it doesn't."

That solution: an overhaul of the Constitution. Major changes. New amendments. We need to get rid of the Electoral College, he says, which twice in recent years has let a minority elect a president. We need to either change how we elect the Senate, a majority of which can be elected by as few as 18 percent of voters. or remove it from the legislative process.

And that's the current situation. A minority elected the president. A minority elected the majority of the senate. A minority decided that the president does not need to obey the law or answer to Congress. The rules of our Constitution have caused the Constitution to fail. It no longer works. So all we need is for a vast majority of Americans to agree to overhaul the Constitution! Let's go! Let's do it! Right?

Fat chance. The people in power are not going to give up that power willingly. And who are those people? A minuscule minority known as "the people with the money."

So what will happen? What is that troublesome rumble I hear just over the horizon?

It's the inevitability of revolution. Mr. Finizio, scholar of history, says that the major changes to the Constitution happen only after cataclysm—first, the revolution of 1776, which resulted in the Constitution and its Bill of Rights; then the Civil War, which was the only way to resolve the issue of slavery.

Mr. Finizio sees the country ripe for revolution. But it will be revolution brewed in the fiery cauldron of necessity, not ideology. The supposedly burgeoning economy is a mirage, a bubble in which 70 percent of Americans don't have $1,000 in the bank. That bubble, inflated by a trillion-dollar deficit, will inevitably burst. Concurrently, climate change will be bringing all sorts of economic hardship, social upheavals, and political strife.

And the nation is armed to the teeth.

The upheaval, he says—that fiery cauldron of necessity—is necessary and inevitable to bring about real change. It is our rendezvous with destiny. The only question is whether it will make things better or worse.

Save that Statue...and the Pedestal

So Mayor Michael Passero is doing to the statue of Columbus what Columbus did to the first Americans he met. He'd going to abscond with it.

The motivations, of course, are different. Columbus wanted a souvenir. He wanted to go back to Europe with evidence that he'd sailed around the world. His proof: genuine "Indians" from India.

Those first few captives were just the beginning of a horrific, long-term atrocity that included mass murder, the enslavement of thousands, and the establishment of a slave-based economic system that would go on for centuries.

I wish I had space here to go into the heart-wrenching details, but I'm also glad I don't. My heart is too readily wrenched.

Less wrenching is the issue of the statue at the corner of Bank and Blinman–Columbus Square, formerly Tyler Square. The statue doesn't have a mother or children, nor does it have dreams, dignity or plans for retirement. Exalted on a pedestal or chained at the ankles, it's all the same to a statue. I don't know what it's made of, but I'm sure it's not flesh, bone and blood. It has no soul.

Mayor Passero wants to abscond with the statue for its own good. I'm quite sure that, being a Democrat, he's opposed to genocide and slavery. He isn't rescuing a murderous slaver. He's rescuing history.

Love him or hate him, Columbus is a significant historical figure. A recent assessment of the 30 most influential people in Western history ranked Columbus #1, and not just for bad reasons. He was way ahead of his time, and except for never recognizing that he hadn't found Asia, he was an excellent navigator. And let's face it, to set sail across an ostensibly infinite ocean–or worse, an ocean with an edge–took some courage.

But just as there are two sides to every story, there are at least two sides to every history. Reducing one side to no side by locking it up in the town garage (or, for that matter, heaving it into the Thames) is not the solution.

Here's a better idea: a Museum of Toppled Statues. The world has plenty that have been or should be torn down–Napoleon, Leopold II, Trotsky, Stalin, Mussolini, Mao, Saddam Hussein, Sha Reza Pahlavi, John Mason, all those Confederate officers and all the horses they rode in on.

Suppose there were a museum where these statues could be preserved and displayed. But instead of standing on pedestals, they'd be chained to facts–detailed narratives, maps, photos, artifacts—in short, the evidence. Both sides of the story. The full history. The truth.

Imagine several dozen stone Columbuses standing in their own museum hall, holding their scrolled maps and globes and looking off toward distant horizons. They'd look like a bunch of overdressed Americans arguing about which way to go—not an atypical scene these days, except for the part about being overdressed.

Imagine Stalin, Mao, and Saddam all puffed up together with their ephemeral, Ozymandian arrogance. Imagine Napoleon scratching his left breast in front of the portrait of Donald Trump in fratty leisurewear. Imagine Lenin shaking that inspiring finger at General Lee's horse.

That, in a nutshell, is what we need: preservation and perspective. Lest we have to watch history repeat once again, let's consider why the statues were erected in the first place, and why they were torn down. If we have to make errors worthy of statues in the future, let's at least try to make different errors.

As Polish aphorist Stanislaw Lec said, "When smashing monuments, save the pedestals—they always come in handy."

I think it would be a sad error to leave What's-his-name's pedestal at What's-his-name's Square without a note about whoever it was who stood there and why he no longer does.

We could then use the pedestal for a statue of the New London Development Corporation. Then we could tear it down and haul it over to the Museum of Toppled Statues, located conveniently nearby in the wasteland around Fort Trumbull.

Might as well haul the pedestal over there, too. But, as Lec recommended, save it. Someday we'll need it. Until then, on the pedestal, let these words appear:

"Look on my Works, ye Mighty, and despair."

On Stuff

It's About Time

Got stuff?

I've sure got stuff. I've got stuff hanging on me like barnacles. Books I love but will never read again. Exotic crafts from faraway lands. Knickknacks and doodads from friends. Antiques passed down from ancestors. Assets worth money if anybody wanted to buy them.

Somehow I have come to need two refrigerators. I have a top-end lawnmower that won't start. Two giant televisions. Antiquated phones. Artwork. A funny sweater that flowed from my mother's fingers. More furniture than I need.

My stuff holds me prisoner. I can't free myself from it. It should be easy, but it's impossible. I don't know if it clings to me or I to it.

Once I dreamed that I came home and found my house burned to the ground. I owned nothing but ashes and an empty lot. I thought, Good.

It isn't just me. Everybody I know has too much stuff. Yes, I know there are people who lack food, need medicine, can't clothe their kids. I know it isn't fair that we accumulate frivolous clutter while they lack necessities, but I don't know what to do about it except say I'm sorry I've spent so much on stuff.

It took me a lifetime to enrich myself with this stuff. Now it turns out that all I really want is time.

Time—that infinite non-commodity that no one has enough of. It's precious, priceless, and unpriced. You can spend time, but you can't buy it.

Time isn't money. Money is time. You can take your money to the mall and trade it for some stuff, but you won't find any time there.

Where can you buy it? Only inside yourself. How do you buy it? With decision. Cash? It's time wasted in a wallet.

I wrote a stupid novel once, a horrid piece of junk, long since recycled into cardboard. But at its core was an interesting idea—a protagonist dedicated to inverting both capitalism and communism. Her premise: we should not be trying to maximize production and consumption. We should be minimizing both and letting free time fill the void.

Time, in her dream, was to replace stuff as the fundamental value of the economy. Free time would be the symbol of status. The wealthy would be those who sat around all day like the people we currently call bums. The poor would be those enslaved by their unenlightened need to keep producing and consuming.

Yes, of course, she knew we'd still need to put time into the production of necessities, but everyone's goal would be to live with as little as possible. People in BMWs would be in envious awe of those who work two days a week and commute on a bike. And those on bikes would feel outdone by those who could afford to saunter.

The climate crisis presses the issue. Less production and consumption means less fuel burned. It gives us more time to solve stuff-born problems.

In some ways, the pandemic lockdown is a dry run of a time-based economy. People are producing less and consuming less, albeit not voluntarily. People have more time, but they feel like they're doing time.

The stuff-based economy has not adjusted to this new way of life. It's still painful. People have learned to live without restaurants and road trips, but they still have to pay rent.

A time-based economy is a revolutionary idea but possible only at the pace of evolution. No mob or army can make it happen over night. It's a shift as big as the transition from feudalism to industrialism. But anyone living above the level of strict necessity can start opting for time over stuff.

The first step is simply decision: to reorient your valuation of wealth.

The stuff-based socio-economic system is inimical to such change. It will do nothing to facilitate. It will resist. But it cannot resist absolutely. You can find small ways to find time, and you can always find small stuff you can live without.

Automation and technology should be helping. We're all producing more per hour than people did 50 years ago, yet we're all working more. Robots are helping, yet the workload worsens. If we'd stuck with the production and stuff that satisfied us 50 years ago, we'd have a twenty-hour workweek today.

But this tectonic-economic shift leaves us with a couple of key questions. What should we do with so much free time? And what would we actually do?

Think about that during your bounty of idle quarantine moments. What would you do if you had half your stuff and twice your time?

Better a Letter

Stuck home and got nothing to do? Write a letter. I mean a regular letter. One of those paper things with your handwriting on it, the kind you fold up and tuck into an envelope, slap a stamp on and spank on its way.

It isn't hard. Get one of those writing sticks like you used back in elementary school. Get the best sheet of paper you can find. If your writing stick is filled with ink, rub the point on the paper until it comes to life. If it's filled with graphite, sharpen it. If you don't have a sharpener, use a knife. Or go down to the Dutch Tavern on Green St. in New London. They have a sharpener on the wall to the left of the men's room, near the "Be Nice or Leave" sign, a rusty old Boston that Eugene O'Neill himself may have used. Turn the crank. Hear it roar.

Sit yourself down. You're doing something important here. Something sacred. You might want to wash your hands first, and not just to free them of germs. The piece of paper you are touching is going to touch someone else. Someone special—special enough to deserve a letter—is going to find your letter in a mailbox, a gem among the junk.

It will be a special moment, rare and beautiful, something warm and human in the cold, corporate slush of ads, catalogs and bills. Fingers will pause. Eyes will light. A short syllable will emit from the lips, a coo of Oh or a gentle Wow, or maybe both.

This letter may outlive you, so put a date and location at the top. Every letter is about "here, now," but someday they become about "back then." Little means more than an old letter.

Start with "Dear," then attach somebody's name, even if it's someone not necessarily worthy of that intimate salutation. "Dear" doesn't necessarily mean you're in love. It also means "Esteemed." Also, "expensive." Also simply "This is a letter to you."

Then a little punctuation. A colon says "Sit up and pay attention!" A comma says, "Sit back and stick with me."

Now you're going to take something out of your head and put it in someone else's head. A very short sentence, just three or four words, is a good way to start. Avoid giving a weather report.

Put a little effort into your penmanship. It may take a while to work the rust from your knuckles. Get swirly. Think of what you can do with a writing stick that you can't with a keyboard. You can go bold in many ways. You can circle words. You can change a dash to an arrow. You can dot an i with a little heart. You can make your exclamation point as fat as a kielbasa. One good question mark can ask more than one question. It can even answer a question.

Write it. Sign your name at the bottom. Fold it up. Crease it well. Maybe touch it with a dot of perfume. Think about the good old days when you could lick the flap and seal it with a kiss. Until further notice, maybe you'd better moisten the flap with a damp towel and just write S.W.A.K. on the back, a little white lie that won't infect anybody.

If you're a hardcore capitalist, you can use a private company to deliver your letter. FedEx will do it for $10.27 if you take it to them. UPS will do it for $8.25, plus another $5 if you want them to come pick it up.

Or you can take advantage of a little socialism. The post office will pick it up at your house and deliver it for 55 cents. For a buck twenty, they'll take it to the other side of the world. And you get to pick the stamp that's right for you—a pretty little picture of flowers, a sea creature, an airplane, a necklace, a hero, a flag, a virgin and her babe, or any of thousands of other images, thousands of reasons people collect stamps.

Oh, if only all of life were as simple as "to get a letter, write a letter." Granted, that's not guaranteed. Some people write back. Some don't. The latter may never get another letter. The former are worth calling "Dear." They will touch you back. The touch will be in your mailbox. Your fingers will pause, and you'll whisper, "Oh" and then "Wow."

Penmanship

I'm trying to improve my penmanship, I really am. It's an embarrassment to me, a burden on recipients of my letters, and a bad sign of the drift of civilization.

I want to abandon my urgent squiggles that stumble forward trying to keep up with my urgent, squiggling thoughts. The proverbial "chicken scratches" describes my squiggles only if the chicken is lost, desperate, terrified and drunk.

My plan: to emulate the wide, looping, almost joyful style of my father's gentle hand. It takes a little longer, but it seems to allow for more thought between the words. I think he enjoyed the craft of it, embellishing his thoughts with flourishes that took their sweet time and enjoyed the journey as much as the destination.

He learned in the days of inclined wooden desks, back when time was slower. The upper right corner of each desk had a hole for an inkwell. I don't think they had special desks for southpaws. Writers wrote with their right or got spanked in the hall.

They dipped their nibs carefully, loading them with enough ink to last a page or so but not so much as to drip. This took time and attention. It allowed a certain reverence for the sacred act of writing. The teacher taught my little father to write loopy, so loopy he wrote, swirling out words like ballerinas on tightropes. He paused at commas, recouped at periods, put special effort into capital letters, had fun with the letters with swooping tails. The form of the words meant almost as much as the meaning of the words.

Or so I imagine. I don't really know, of course, but my first desk in the first grade had a hole for an inkwell. We were told there would be no more fountain pens. Even then, little I sensed the passing of an era. We were given pencils but we weren't told why.

Fountain pens had a certain classiness, but pencils had their advantages. For one thing, if you made a mistake, you could erase it with the rubbery little delete button at the top of the pencil. Pens, on the other hand, did not allow for error. One had to think ahead, not count on cleaning up one's mistakes—a lesson I sorely needed and still do.

For another thing, everybody had to make periodic trips to the pencil sharpener, typically a Boston bolted to a wall. Classrooms were pretty quiet in those days, so the roaring grind of steel against cedar and graphite was a veritable act of defiance. One could get in trouble for joy-grinding.

And once in a while, the gut of the pencil sharpener had to be emptied—yet another opportunity for noise—bang-bang-bang-bang-bang on the inside of a steel waste basket.

(Another classroom chore that's gone the way of grinding pencils: clapping the erasers. Oh what joy for any girl or boy to get to go outside and clap up a white cloud of chalk dust–a public service entrusted only to the dependable and well behaved, usually a girl.)

I think it was junior high school when they entrusted us with ball point pens. Again, they didn't explain why. They (I'm looking at you, Mrs. Sparks) insisted, with unabashed absurdity, that errors be not scratched out but erased. In the case of ink, that meant rubbing a hole through the paper.

Only now do I understand that that was a lesson in life, a lesson far more important than penmanship or (nice try, Mrs. Sparks) diagraming sentences. The lesson: no matter how stupid something is, you have to do it the way they tell you to do it.

Now I'm back to fountain pens. I have more than I can use, some cheap, some classy, some from Europe, some inherited, some from flea markets and tag sales. I have a few posted in the spots where I'm likely to write a letter. I try to give them all a turn. They all look so eager, so born-to-write. I don't want to neglect one. I've never heard a fountain pen cry, and I hope I never do.

My hand is unworthy of these fine pens, their iridium nibs, their secret pasts, their highlights of silver and gold. They slow me down– not enough, but they're trying. They're taming me. Stop squiggling, they tell me. Try loopy. Hold me gently and make me swirl.

How about the Some News We Can Use

I'm getting tired of the national numbers on the TV news—the ups and downs of the NASDAQ, the nudges to the prime rate, how much we spent on Black Friday, the infinitesimal blips in the wholesale price index.

I don't want numbers about numbers. I want numbers about people—people who live around here. I want to hear about today's variation in the average number of children in New London classrooms. I want to know what percent of our sixth-graders can, today, find Iraq and Paraguay on a map. I want to know the New London High School drop-out total for this week, this month, this year-to-date compared with last year. I'd like to see totals comparing New London with Waterford, Bridgeport, Hartford and Greenwich.

I'm not interested in the S&P 500. I'm interested in the change in infant mortality in New London County since the last election. I want to know how many people went to the L&M emergency room with asthma attacks this week. I want to see how many people came down with cancer in Southeast Connecticut in the past 12 months, and I wouldn't mind a color-coded map showing me where they live.

I don't want hourly reports on the Dow Jones Industrial Average. I want hourly reports on air pollution levels along I-95, sulfur-dioxide emissions from each Connecticut power plant, radiation readouts from the seawater outside Millstone Nuclear Power Station.

I don't care what the Fed said. I want a daily report on how many in New London County have been hit with bullets, year-to-date, with pie charts comparing family income, skin color, Smarter Balanced Assessment scores, and caliber. With each increase, I'd like to see a map showing where the body fell and where the governor, the mayor, and the head of the Fed were standing at the time.

I know it doesn't matter where they were standing, but neither does the NASDAQ. In fact, I'd like to see a graph that correlates changes in the NASDAQ and changes in any local parameter.

I don't want to know what the president blithered. I want to hear local officials report on what they did yesterday. I want to know what they're worried about this year as opposed to last year. I want to know how the members of the city counsel voted.

I'd like to see a line graph showing me how many people in New London and Connecticut declared bankruptcy today, this week, this month, this year, due to health problems. I'd like to see these numbers graphed in comparison with the profits of insurance companies and the compensation of their CEOs.

I don't want to see the temperatures in a dozen cities, all within three degrees of each other. I want to see what percent of their homes are under foreclosure and how many residents are behind on their taxes.

I want to know how many elementary school students in this city need psychiatric drugs to get them through the day. I want see the trend in the average weight of 8th-graders. I want to know how many kids are homeless. I want to hear each and every principal answer three hard questions.

I'd like to accompany daily changes in Connecticut's average hourly wages. I'd like a news anchor to report the day-by-day changes in the gap between per capita incomes in Greenwich and New London. I'd really like to know the average number of hours people spent on the job yesterday versus a year ago, ten years ago, and fifty years ago.

It should be easy to report changes in the number of people receiving public assistance. It might be a little harder to determine the number of corporations receiving public assistance, but we could do it if we wanted.

Would it be hard to issue weekly reports on the rates of divorce, adoption, foster care, one-parent families, teen pregnancies, and abortion? I'd like to know today's percentage of people who wished they lived in another neighborhood, city, or state, percentage of families in poverty, percentage of families with more money than anyone could morally spend on themselves.

If society can keep track of the Dow, the S&P, the GDP, the inflation rate, the slot take at the casinos, consumer spending, and temperatures throughout the land, then we can keep track of, and report on, data reflecting the human condition. Our focus and priorities are clearly misguided. Would anyone care to guess why?

Alarm Clock

Up at the northern frontier of the Day's coverage area, just beyond the reach of home delivery, Hanover Congregational Church holds an annual auction. People bid on other people's stuff, stuff not long ago new, now just shy of antique. Whatever doesn't get sold at the auction gets laid out on tables a week later in the parish house for a tag sale that can't be beat. That's where I picked up an alarm clock for an affordable 25 cents.

I'm a pathological tightwad, so wresting a quarter from my sweaty palm isn't easy. But this clock was the real thing. It's the kind you get to wind up every day, the kind that goes tick-teck-tick-teck-tick at the pace my mother's heart went while I was biding my time in utero and she was in a movie theater watching Godzilla destroy Tokyo. Or maybe it was cops and robbers. I don't know. I was asleep, floating as if in a dream. Once in a while I'd roll over.

What I mean to say is, it was a clock that would lull me through sleep with the assurance that one tick-teck will be followed by another and another as I dreamed in all good comfort. Assurance and predictability are important in clocks and mothers both.

I love my mother, and I love my little alarm clock. Westclox named it "Baby Ben," alluding to royal ancestry. Baby Ben doesn't stop when the lights go out. It doesn't even care. And it doesn't awaken me with a pushy electronic hoot-hoot-hoot-hoot. Rather, it chortles with the muted ring of a little bell, a subtle percussion that doesn't necessarily want to start a fight. It doesn't tell me I have to wake up. It just tells me I should.

Down at the bottom of the dial, in the curve of a grim smile, three rare words appear, tiny-weeny but upper case: MADE IN USA. I don't quite know how to take those words. Are they a resonant statement of pride or a ghostly reminder of bygone glory? I don't know, but I'll use it as an excuse to mention that my mother, too, was MADE IN USA. Kentucky.

Baby Ben has a face shaped like the window of a 1959 rocket ship. Its numbers, with their tiny, squarish serifs, may once have passed for futuristic. Its hands—one big, one little—glow in the dark. So do the numbers and the sixty little minute marks. It's an analog clock, so when the time is 3:56, I don't have to think my way to the conclusion that it's almost four o'clock. I just look at the hands and know how far from four o'clock I am. Likewise, the clock doesn't deign to tell me whether I'm dealing with a.m. or p.m. It doesn't think I'm stupid. Just like my mother, it expects me to know.

The glow is a soft, pale, radium blue. It respects the darkness of a bedroom. The glow fades during the night. When I can't see it anymore, I know it's almost time to get up. But not yet. The actual time is: time to roll over.

And I don't go thinking I can set the alarm to, precisely, say, 6:30. No, I can set it to about 6:30. If it feels like ringing at 6:38 or 6:22, and my day is subsequently a mess, it isn't because of the clock. It's because my life was already a mess. Just as my mother said it would be if I don't get out of bed. Which I do, just as soon as Baby Ben says I'm ready.

Federal Snow Days: It's about Time.

I'm disappointed that none of the Democratic primary candidates has mentioned a certain injustice that afflicts at least half the nation. All across the South and up the Pacific coast, millions of people are denied the possibility of a snow day.

As the climate catastrophe worsens, the line between snow-day states and no-snow-date states moves north. It seems to have reached Connecticut already. I can't remember the last time we had a decent blizzard.

By "decent blizzard" I mean the kind that keeps everyone at home for a couple of days while Mother Nature reminds us who's in charge; the kind that makes cars look like burial mounds; the kind that makes TV meteorologists wet their pants with the urgency of their exaggerated predictions.

Ideally, the lights go out, and the internet goes down. Candles get lit. Families hunker under blankets and remember why houses used to have fireplaces. They talk to each other. They snooze in the afternoon. They know tomorrow's going to be an agony of old-fashioned shovel-based drudgery. But until then, there's nothing to do but nothing.

Snow days are a good thing, and never have we needed them more. We need down-time, dead-time, do-nothing time. We need to unplug our brains so we can contemplate the things whose motion is otherwise too slow to notice. We need to visit the place where clocks have no meaning.

We need a snow day just to think about why we no longer have snow days. Their extinction isn't as serious as the flooding of Florida, the burning of California, the roasting of Texas, or the lashings of wintertime tornados, but still: there will come a day when snow days are nothing more than the lore of grandparents, like legends of one-horse open sleighs.

We could prevent a lot of those disasters if we tried, but it seems we just aren't going to. But the snow-day problem we can easily solve. By a simple act of Congress, we can mandate a number of randomly assigned snow days each year.

Federal snow days don't have to involve snow, and if one of them happens to fall in July, well, that wouldn't be such a bad thing, would it? Nothing to shovel. No pipes to freeze. The only rule is: you have to stay home and hope the lights don't go out. Which, if I'm in charge, is going to happen. Whole neighborhoods, even whole towns, are going to lose their lights—exactly as they did back when we let blizzards make that decision. The big difference: predictability. You'll have days or weeks to get your candles together, stock up on toilet paper, get a book out of the library, and be glad you don't have to remember where you left your snow shovel. And the weatherman won't have to change his pants during commercial breaks.

I'm going to suggest ten as a good number of snow days each year, though there are bigger numbers I'd be glad to consider. One a month would be nice.

In fact, if elected to the throne, I will declare a four-day workweek with Wednesdays off so we can attend to life's problems, by which I don't mean snow. I mean taking kids to the beach or a ballgame. I mean knit an afghan, make a nice meal, have coffee with a neighbor, weed a garden, read a book, or attend to your local democracy. I mean go to bed early and sleep late.

Ultimately, I mean quell the national insanity—whatever it is that's driving people to shoot strangers, resort to opioids, use pills to control children, kill themselves, eat their way to diabetic obesity, or succumb to any of the many other manifestations of psychological malaise. It's getting bad out there. It isn't the guns or the pills, the cell phones or the hyperactive children or the ubiquitous corn syrup. It's the nonstop speed of things. We are running out of time. That's what we need. We need more time.

Summer School vs. Summer Slide

An astute reader in Norwich recently sent a letter to the editor of The Day. He suggested something that a lot of people have been thinking about for a long time.

His idea: school all year round.

My idea: use year-round education to expand curriculums.

Year-round school doesn't mean more days in school. It means shorter summer vacations and more days off during other months.

The advantages are many:

• The big one: kids avoid the "summer slide" when they forget a lot of what they learned before summer vacation.

• Teachers avoid burnout with more breaks from their difficult and demanding jobs.

• Kids don't spend a long, boring summer away from friends.

• More outdoor school activities are possible.

• More flexibility for smaller classes, school resources, curriculum, sports programs, and remote instruction.

• Teachers may have a chance to work extra days and make extra pay.

And let's remember why we have a long summer vacation. The tradition goes back to the agricultural economy. Kids were released from school so they could work on the farm.

Gone are the days when families needed child labor in the field. Today the need is for citizens who are not just well educated but broadly educated. They need skills for jobs, of course, but they also need more contact with nature, experience in gardening and other outdoor activities, opportunities for leadership, and more vigorous exercise and group play outdoors.

Summers are good for such an expansion of curriculums. School would be a lot more interesting if kids spent more time outdoors. And they're less likely to get bored if their school week is only four days and every month includes a short break.

There's a big disadvantage to losing the traditional summer break. It eliminates or reduces other educational opportunities, such as family vacations, summer camp, and engaging in the kind of play that makes childhood fun.

But take a look at what actually happens. Take a drive through a residential neighborhood in the middle of July. Count the number of children who are playing outdoors. It's probably about the same as the number of children working in fields.

And how many summer days are really dedicated to family vacations? How many weeks are spent at camp (by those who can afford it)? How many of these activities could be taken care of in a three-week vacation and a summer of four-day weekends? How much of the summer is spent in front of a computer screen or television?

Needless to say, any such change in the school year would require a lot of creative thinking and changes in traditional family plans. But for every necessary change there are innumerable alternatives and opportunities.

Families could still take vacations, and vacations approved as educational could replace certain school time. School could include summer camps with an educational focus.

Meanwhile, kids remaining at school would enjoy smaller classes and more attention.

Lots of short, scattered breaks opens opportunities for remedial classes and tutorials for kids who aren't keeping up. They also allow for special enrichment experiences, such as class trips, preparation for tests, organized volunteerism, and special class projects.

The COVID-19 crisis has taught us that we can adapt, that we can find creative solutions, and that the solutions can be valuable even after the original problem has been solved.

We should be applying the same ingenuity to education. I think everyone recognizes that our system of education has problems. It isn't as bad as some people think, but it could sure use some improvement.

The complete reorganization required for year-round school opens possibilities for many solutions.

American schools aren't as bad as many think, but according to the U.N.'s Programme for International Student Assessment, which assesses what students actually know, we aren't in the world's top 10. Our dreams of greatness are all on vacation.

In that most other countries use year-round education, we would be wise to consider rethinking our antiquated scheduling, and we should look for ways to use a new annual schedule to make new advances in preparing today's kids for tomorrow's world.

Paean to Pawnshops

I never pass up a pawnshop. They all contain mysteries and untold stories. No two are the same, though they all share a certain spirit.

In other words, pawnshops are like people—each unique and filled with their special collection of jewels, junk, oddities and backstories.

It would be too easy to say that pawnshops are the place where dreams go to die. Yes, some do—the guitars hanging by their necks behind the counter, each a dead dream of stardom. The beds of rings under glass, each with secret meaning reduced to memory. The fetish knives, so creatively lethal but unbloodied. Old tools—drills, sanders, nail guns, equipment for some reason no longer needed.

But as the National Pawnbrokers Association hastens to point out, pawnshops are oases of hope—desperate hope, yes, over-the-hump hope, yes, but that's when hope's worth the most. A pawnshop is a quick loan collateralized with something less necessary than a tank of gas, a bottle of medicine, a down payment on the rent, a bus ticket to somewhere better.

Pawnshops are the last safety net for 55 million people classified as—rather coldly, I think— the "underbanked." In fact, almost eight percent of Americans are utterly unbanked. No checking account, no savings, and all they can get out of a loan officer is a muffled guffaw. Mississippi ranks first in unbankedness; Connecticut ranks 21st.

I don't like to think of myself as "banked," but I guess that's one of many words for me. (Thank you, Chelsea-Groton, for your patience and understanding.) So a pawnshop, to me, is more of a cross between a museum and a yard sale. This is where I'm going to get an unparalleled peek at a side of the world that's pretty much inaccessible to the banked. I might also find that certain something special that can't be found at Walmart or a mall.

I'd always assumed that the word "pawn" derived from the defenseless and dispensable chess piece, itself related to "peon," the commoner, the laborer, a word going back to the Latin for foot soldier.

But no. It comes from an Old French word, possibly from an Old German word referring to a pledge or something given as security. It could also refer to booty or plunder. Or, I suppose, stolen goods.

Pawn's only synonym is "hock," derived from a Dutch word, "hok," referring to a jail or pen. Understandably, it became slang for debt. If you can't see the connection, go find an unbanked person and ask how deep debt feels.

And if you happen to be a burglar with stolen goods to fence, first of all, thank you for reading The Day. Second of all, don't be stupid. Don't take your pelf to a pawn shop. Every pawnshop can enter a serial number or description into a national database of stolen goods. The pawnshop will quickly discover whether you lifted that laptop in Reno. Also, you'll get your picture taken.

Philip Pavone, owner of AZ Pawn in Norwich, says he isn't interested in stolen goods even though business has been slow. Sales were brisk for a while as people snapped up anything that would make the quarantined life more sufferable—TVs, laptops, video games and such.

But lately there's been a drop-off of desperados coming in for emergency loans. Pavone lays the blame on the stimulus checks that families are receiving. For many, especially the underbanked with lots of kids, they've never had so much income. Their gas tanks are full. They've got their meds, their rent and no reason to leave town. No need to hock their dreams; they have enough to live on, at least for now.

Consider the Couch

I am the only person I know who's too lazy to sit on the couch and watch TV. I lack the requisite energy. By the time I figure out how to work the remote, I'm ready for a nap.

But that doesn't mean I don't respect the sofa. In these times of quarantined boredom, the living room couch is a lifeboat in a sea of contagion. It's a good reason to stay home.

Couch? Sofa? What's the difference?

Good question. Geography is a partial but inadequate explanation. "Couch" has been more traditional in North America, Australia, and Ireland. Yet in those countries' motherland, "sofa" predominates. In South America, it's pronounced "sofá."

A more complete answer lies in history and etymology–the source of the words. The Norman invasion of 1066 brought the word "couche" from France, where it derived from the verb "coucher," to lie down. This was furniture that the English had been sorely lacking.

The word in modern French, however, is "canapé." That word in English, of course, refers to a type of hors d'oeuvre. The derivation is understandable. A slab of fish on a tuft of bread bears an uncanny resemblance to a couch potato poised for an early season ballgame.

Sofa, on the other hand, comes from an Arabic word pronounced "suffa," referring to a bench or ledge. Yes, Arabic, the language that also gave us "ottoman," "alcohol" and "zero."

In Aramaic–language Jesus spoke–the word was "sippa," though it referred to something more like a mat. It is interesting to note that in the New Testament's only reference to Jesus sleeping, he was sacked out on what was arguably a rudimentary sofa. (Mark 4:35-41)

Given the historical roots of couch and sofa, one could say that a couch is for lying on, the sofa more for sitting on. So a couch would reside in the privacy of the living room, while a sofa would be found in the parlor for chats with guests.

And as long as we're on that topic, let me clarify: one lies, not lays, on a couch, unless one is a chicken, in which case, please, do it outside.

The word most common in anglophone Canada is "chesterfield," named after Philip Stanhope, 4th Earl of Chesterfield, who commissioned one for his sedentary preferences—leather, dimpled, and low-slung. Whether those preferences explain his two illegitimate sons is not known, but it should be noted that at one point he held the position of Lord of the Bedchamber.

(Yes, recent grads, that is an actual job. But openings are few, and appointment by Royal Warrant is much more a matter of who, not what, you know.)

Astute readers are by now wondering what the deal is with the "fainting couch." Contrary to common presumption, it has nothing to do with falling unconscious on a designated divan.

The fainting couch is identifiable by a high back at one end, sometimes wrapping around the side. It accommodated a person with a need to sit up while somewhat stretched out. During Victorian times, it was used to treat women suffering from "hysteria." The treatment involved a "manual pelvic massage" by a doctor or, depending on preference, midwife.

If you think Covid-19 is bad, be glad you weren't alive during the hysteria epidemic. It was so common that houses often had a fainting room for the fainting couch. The medical procedure often had to be applied weekly, sometimes for an hour or more. The fainting room ensured privacy while the specially designed couch facilitated proper posture.

So whether you have a couch, sofa, canapé, divan, futon, or daybed, show it some respect. Appreciate its loyalty. Thank it for being there. Give it a pat on the back. Do what Jesus did: take a nap.

Take the Corporate Out of Christmas

I am a pathological penny-pincher. My parents were depression babies, and they made sure I was, too. They handed off the tightwad baton. I turn off lights when I leave a room. I hang my laundry. I turn down the heat. I warm up my leftovers and clean my plate. I get my money's worth out of a paper towel.

And on Black Friday, I fail to do my patriotic duty. This year, while others shopped the internet in desperate consumerism, I boiled the carcass of a turkey and added the leftover onions, green beans, carrots and potatoes. I made dumplings from the stuffing.

"Black Friday" sounds ominous, like a date night with Darth Vader. I prefer an alternative: Buy Nothing Day.

BND doesn't demand much. You can sleep late, can take a walk, catch up on your reading, never contributing a dime to the GNP of China.

Folks in a few states — Rhode Island was the first — hold a Buy Nothing Coat Exchange event. Rather than shop, people bring used winter coats to a central location and exchange them for something "new." People without coats can come get one.

When you buy something at a store or from Amazon, you're sending your money to a distant corporation that sends a lot of it to the other side of the world. Every purchase involves the consumption of natural resources and the burning of fossil fuel. On top of that, you're buying not just a product but a whole lot of packaging that has to be dealt with.

The downside of buying largely disappears when you make something yourself or buy something second hand. And if you buy from a local producer, your money stays close to home and doesn't involve much packaging. Buying art and crafts may be the most generous kind of purchase. The consumption of resources is minimal, the money stays local, an artist or artisan is encouraged, the world becomes a more beautiful place and the gift is treasured for its human touch.

In many towns, you may be able to give away or acquire something for free through the Buy Nothing organization. Most towns have a Buy Nothing group on Facebook. People list things they want to give away or things they need. You can find your local group at buynothingproject.org. The New London group, which has over 600 members, has a Foody Friday where some people can thin out their pantries and others can find food they can't afford. Someone in the 783-member Norwich group set up a food pantry on her porch.

Christmas doesn't have to be – and sure shouldn't be – an orgy of acquisition, consumption, profit and plastic. Generosity is a fundamental Christian precept, but glitter isn't. Buying local, buying used, giving away, and making it yourself are at the core of Christmas.

'Tis the season of tightwads. Hallelujah!

E-Muggers and Other Muggers

I can't keep track of how many times a day people try to rob me. But if there's been any recent advance in civilization, it's that robbery no longer has to involve the antiquated violence of mugging.

Thanks to the miracle of the internet, e-muggers can reach out to millions of people at a time. Just today I've received a tempting offer from a bogus insurance company, an alert about my credit rating, a heartfelt request for mutual assistance from a wealthy Nigerian widow, congratulations from Walmart, some shocking news that Big Pharma doesn't want me to know, more shocking news about melting belly fat, a chance to win $5,000 a week for life, several jobs in the Dallas area, a credit card I've never heard of, a free vacuum cleaner, the TRUTH about vaccines, a slew of exclusive VIP invitations, and a reminder that my Trump life membership is about to expire.

Yes, a life membership that expires. How do I know it's really from Trump and not some e-mugger? Because "life membership" in a person sounds like conman fast-talk, and the self-contradiction of an expiring life membership is shamelessly blatant. And who but he would send a follow-up email offering me Gold membership for as little as $25?

And that's not all! That's just the e-mugger messages. At least as many come from vigilant corporations stabbing in the dark for my supposed needs. Somehow a chain of shoe stores knows I need new shoes. What it doesn't know is that I don't want new shoes.

And despite the theoretical accuracy of artificially intelligent algorithms, if somebody thinks I'm in the market for furniture, they are barking up the wrong tree. I don't buy furniture. I leave furniture at the curb and feel wealthier for the empty space it left behind.

I don't know who's in charge of this Amazonian gush of sales pitches. Sometimes I suspect it's nobody. And I'm not sure whether that's good or bad. The lack of productive purpose hints at a lack of leadership and organization. On the other hand, I'm glad they aren't organized.

None of this bothers me too terribly much. I go through my email as if cleaning a fish, quickly discarding the yucky parts while preserving the real meat.

I can afford to ignore it all because I'm pretty much impervious to sales pitches. I have all the stuff I want plus a lot of stuff I don't. I have reached the frontier of spending. My wad is wound tight. I'm not buying anything I can't eat or read.

Maybe it's my own felonious tendencies that helps me spot scams. I confess I've put some thought into ripping off Nigerian widows. I bet I could rob a bank if I felt like it. And if I could find the suckers who buy Gold memberships in Donald Trump, I'd be glad to sell them the EXCLUSIVE secret to melting belly fat. (It's an ancient Egyptian formula PROVEN to be effective because have you ever seen an overweight hieroglyphic? No, you haven't.)

But the felony of the day is tax fraud. Now's the time. The ability of the IRS to detect tax cheats has been choked back by 20 percent over the last ten years. It's so short-staffed that it can barely process tax returns, let along figure out who's cheating.

One thing the Service has figured out, however, is that it's easier to nail the lower class than the upper class. Those who labor for a living tend to have all their income documented. Those who do whatever it is the rich do tend to have convoluted streams of income and complex, if not shady, schemes of deduction. The IRS estimates that 99 percent of taxes due on labor are paid. Compliance on shiftier income is estimated at just 45 percent.

And of course it's easier to "process" the poor than the billionaire with a phalanx of lawyers and a coven of accountants. The poor are the low-hanging fruit.

I don't see much difference between old-fashioned muggers, e-muggers, and tax muggers, except that tax muggers cause everyone else's taxes to go up. President Biden has proposed beefing up the IRS for better enforcement. I think it's about time.

People and Places

How Art Abides

Bess Gaby, director of New London's Hygienic Art organization, doesn't want to hear about "starving artists," not as a business model.

Arts organizations in New London are, in fact, getting hungry under pandemic pressures, but pleas of starvation aren't going to solve the problem. Bess has a better idea: collaboration and community.

Bess is new to the job. She became director in February, just a month before the virus hit the fan. She expected a nice job, not a trial by fire.

Bess is an artist, and, like most artists who prefer to avoid starvation, she took a tour through commercial art. But she was happy to get back to the real thing. She became a resident artist at the Hygienic, and a few months later she became director.

And then things started to fall apart. Covid spread. Events were canceled. Volunteers had to stay home. The gallery closed. Grants became as iffy as the projects and programs that weren't happening.

New London's other big arts organization, the Eastern Connecticut Symphony Orchestra, had the same kinds of problems. The situation couldn't get much worse for both organizations. The deck was stacked against them, and old solutions weren't going to work.

The one thing they had going for them was art.

Artists have a propensity for new ideas. They evolve in unprecedented directions. It's what they do.

It's also what the young do. Art and evolution are inherent to the spirit of youth. The young are restless and ready to try something–anything–new. They reject convention. They still have hope.

Fortunately, the New London arts organizations were being led by the young. Caleb Bailey, executive director of the ECSO, was 35. Bess was younger than that. They were ready to reject convention and try something–anything–new. They didn't see doom. They saw opportunity.

One convention they rejected was the grabbing of all the grants they could, even at the other's expense. They also saw the pointlessness of trying to hoard their respective audiences.

They had a better idea, an adaptation whose time had come. They wouldn't compete. They would collaborate. By sharing resources and constituencies, they could both thrive.

Thus was born the Soundscape concerts at the Hygienic Art Park. After five months of isolation and quarantine, it was just what the community needed. Musicians had an outdoor performance space (and jobs). The Hygienic was enabling art. And the community had what it desperately needed: social gatherings at free concerts in sunlight and fresh air.

For the sake of social distancing, only a minimal audience was allowed into the park. But then something unexpected happened. People gathered outside the Bank Street gate. People watched from a rooftop. People took pictures. The events seemed fabulous and unreal, and they had repercussions beyond the park fence.

The spirit of collaboration extended to the Hot on Bank yoga studio. Like most other businesses, it was closed until someone realized that yoga could be practiced outdoors and that wellness of body and spirit were part of art.

The Art Park was also home to the Drop In day camp of the Drop-In Community Learning and Resource Center. "The Drop" offers programs for children.

Bess Gaby's concept of collaboration went on beyond traditional art communities. She recognized that workers at Electric Boat were engaged in creative, innovative pursuits—design, video, engineering, information technology, and all sorts of craftsmanship. Putting a boat under water is an art, and the people who make it possible often like to look beyond the strictly technical aspects of their jobs.

Taking advantage of Zoom technology, Bess is pulling together an impressive five-part series of lectures and discussions on art and innovation, Creative Cooperative City. It pulled together artists, teachers, thinkers, engineers, business people, and other fringes of the arts community.

The future of the Hygienic is unclear. It will be there, of course, but its most popular programs—the Salon des Independents, the Naked Canvas, the Mayfly plays, the fashion show, the poetry readings and other events—might not be able to brighten the winter as they used to.

But something will happen. Artists are in charge. Ain't no virus gonna out-evolve them. It's going to be different, and it's going to be good.

Dunn's Art in Plain Sight

Carol Dunn's brother invited her to do a little fishing on the Sound.

It didn't take long for him to regret the invitation. They'd just passed under the railway bridge in Mystic when she shouted, "Wait! Stop! Go back!"

"What?"

"Go back. Under the bridge..."

And there she started taking pictures of some peeling paint. Some rusty bolts. Old nails.

Along came another boat. A lady hollers over, "What's the problem?"

"It's OK," the brother said. "She's just a little crazy. She's an artist."

Such is Carol Dunn's life and vision of the world. She gets ambushed by beauty.

It's everywhere, in every cloud, every stone, any given leaf, a patch of rust, a fishing lure...

Case in point: a friend fell down some stairs. Dunn went to visit, and she saw something ineffably beautiful in the bandages, the stitches, the bruise and dried blood – not in the pain those things represent, but in their abstract, meaningless colors and forms.

She took the photos to her home studio on Hanover Pond in Sprague, tinkered with them in an app or two, tried this and that and a couple other things, ended up producing a variety of unidentifiable images, each intriguing in its own way.

So goes the life and eye of Carol Dunn. She's attuned to beauty, the beauty within the ordinary. She sees through meaning to glean the unadulterated aesthetic behind it.

Hence the title of Dunn's Norwich Arts Center exhibit – "In Plain Sight." The exhibit is open to the public from Nov. 6 until the end of the month.

Her work falls into three categories.

One is unaltered photography, simply things she's seen that less crazy people might miss – the lines and colors of fishing lures, the ravages of rust, the time in weathered woodgrain, stains on a wall, a vision through a foggy window, the uncelebrated stories of sidewalk tiles and slates people have walked over without seeing.

She also alters photography, using software to render the plain into something surreal or recast it to look like not just what it is but what it isn't yet.

Dunn's photography extends to photopolymer etching, a process of transferring a picture – altered or original – to a sheet of steel, then inking prints from it.

She also finds elements of art in the mundane and unadvertised.

One such assemblage, "The Space Between," is a framed hodgepodge of folding carpentry rulers and a few nails. Another, "Earth, Wind, Fire," consists of three old bottles, one containing dirt, another wisps of milkweed, another a burnt match and charred paper.

Dunn's interest in photography goes back to when it cost money. She was in the third grade when she aimed an Instamatic, ever so parsimoniously, at interesting subjects.

She put a lot of thought into the single shot she could afford, cropping with the lens rather than in a darkroom.

The darkroom came later, after a career track one wouldn't expect to precede fine art.

She started as a student intern in a prison. She went on to become a corrections officer, then a rehab counselor, and ultimately warden of the Janet S. York Correctional Institution in Niantic.

It would hardly seem the realm of art, but Dunn saw a certain beauty in her charges. She says it was a "wonderful career" where she could intervene to help people – not just inmates but staff. (Her caring and humanistic approach to incarceration is explored in a book, "The Farm: Life Inside a Women's Prison," by Andi Rierden.)

Once she got out of prison, so to speak, she turned to what would seem to be the polar opposite – the world of beauty, most of it found outdoors.

Besides art, Dunn loves winning awards for her art. The list on her website, caroldunnart.com, is a couple yards long.

She also likes selling her art – the money, sure, yes, of course, but also the confirmation of having her work on someone's wall. She likes to endow a certain nobility to the peeled paint of a rusting bridge. She likes people to see what she sees, maybe see that she isn't so crazy after all.

Once Upon a T

Herb Savage's Model T isn't a show car. It's what he drives to town, to the dump, to visit friends. It's his car, or rather, his pick-up. It was built in 1924, four years after Savage himself was built.

Savage invited me to go visit a guy named Gumbs up in Canterbury. I was glad to go. I'd never ridden in a T before and never met a guy named Gumbs.

Savage and his best friend Suzie picked me up in Hanover on the first day of November. Suzie rode in back for the elbow room; I rode in front for the full T experience, which in Savage's T includes a lot of fresh air. Bombing down Canterbury's Walker Road, a woodsy shortcut with grass down the middle and puddles deeper than they look, the experience comes to include water splashing up over the windshield.

Savage doesn't coddle his T. Walker Road's nothing to a car that's been around since Calvin Coolidge was president and Babe Ruth was king.

Sitting shoulder-to-shoulder with Savage, I realize that driving a T is a lot like riding a horse. It depends more on feel and persuasion than on gauges and control.

It's also a lot like knitting while doing the foxtrot. You shift from low to high with a pedal on the left, brake with a pedal on the right, throw it into reverse with the pedal in the middle, accelerate with the fingers of your right hand while tending to the timing with the fingers of your left while your hands in the middle keep the car dancing in a pretty straight line.

Thirty miles an hour is plenty fast in a car like this. You can exchange words with bicyclists as you pull around them. You can notice the color of a falling leaf. You can give a squirrel a chance to change its mind. You can honk to people raking in the yard, and the people have time to take a hand off their rakes and wave.

People love to wave at a Model T, and Savage loves to honk. It's a good honk, a honk that goes way back.

Savage doesn't just have a Model T. He practically is a Model T. He drove his first at the age of 9, when he used his father's to spread manure on a field off Savage Road in Preston. He bought his own for $2 at the age of 12.

He was 23 when he joined the army, 24 when he found himself standing on the radioactive rubble of Hiroshima, a flat desert with a few scorched skeletons of buildings. It was quite a sight for a kid from the fields of eastern Connecticut.

He remembers the burnt wheels of trolleys that had been blown apart. He doesn't remember thinking that maybe technology had gone too far.

We sputter past the hay fields of Woodchuck Hill and the woods of Bates Pond, around the switchbacks of Gooseneck Hill, over the Quinebaug at Butts Bridge, and into the embrace of the yellow maples that arch over Barstow.

Marty Gumbs has a farm and welding shop there. Savage drops the tailgate so Suzie can hop down.

Gumbs has a new 1926 pick-up out of Wisconsin Rapids. An old timer had traded it in on something a little newer, and the used car dealer put it up to auction on eBay.

On the basis of six pictures and testimony that the thing ran, Gumbs took it with a bid of $5,000. For $900 he got it trucked to Canterbury.

Savage puts his lanky fingers to the black paint and says, "I'd say you've got a nice car here."

Nice but not perfect. The oil filter leaks a little, and one tire looks too busted for hope. It went flat up in Plainfield on Gumbs' first ride. Now it's off the rim and he can't get it back on.

That's the main reason Savage's here. A person can change a Model T tire with just a couple of screwdrivers if a person knows how, but Gumbs isn't one of those people. He apologizes, says he's just a beginner at this. Savage says, "We all were once. We all had to learn. That's why I'm here."

So he's here to fix a flat and teach somebody how. But he's also here for mysterious reasons that relate to Suzie, Hiroshima, knitting, leaf rakes, the good honk, and the way the world's going.

Savage says Gumbs' car is a rare case of an original: original motor on its original chassis. At some point in the last 80 years the floor of the truck bed was replaced with plywood, but Gumbs is going to pull it out, put in "something more authentic."

He's going to get some spare condensers, too. Savage tells him to look for old ones. They aren't so flimsy.

It takes four hands to start Gumb's T: one for the timing lever, one for the gas lever, one for the choke, one for something under the hood.

Gumbs tries it twice. The motor coughs a few times but doesn't catch. Savage sets the choke just so and says to try it again. At a precise moment between the second and third cough, his hand darts from the engine to the choke, snaps it in, darts back to the engine. It clears its throat, mutters something that sounds like yes, and settles into the quiet, confident sputter of a good car ready to go somewhere.

Savage folds his bones down to pick up Suzie and ease her into the back of his T. She's a little gray at the muzzle but has a lot of miles left in her.

Savage pulls the wooden stopper from the milk can he keeps on his running board, tilts it to Suzie so she can lap up a little water. She sticks half her head in there and laps a lot, her tail steady with concentration.

Her lapping echoes in the half-empty can. Savage holds it till she's done.

Listen to Your Mother Goose

Once upon a long, long time ago, after day was done, the sun gone down, people squatted around their home entertainment system to hear someone tell a story. In the flames they saw the story unfold—an ancestor who was brave, a child who didn't listen, a frog who fell in love, a god who wreaked revenge.

The stories were illustrated with no more than trembles of voice, the emulation of a sob, gestures and shadows in orange flame light, maybe a song, maybe the prop of a stone or a spear.

The stories did more than entertain. They transplanted memory and preserved a kind of history. They turned legend into a kind of truth. They passed on values. They knitted complexity into cultures and cinched communities closer.

People told stories for a hundred millennia before anyone wrote or read a story. And despite books, television, movies, and the internet, we still tell stories. They come in genres known as gossip, ghost stories, bar talk, speeches, radio dramas, public relations, political spin, sales pitches, smooth-talk, desperate excuses, and job interviews.

Back when I was a camp counselor, I used to thrill my little campers with stories around a campfire, just as in Paleolithic times. I was good at it. Too good. I could set up a horror story so real that, at a climactic moment, kids would scream as they lurched toward the fire. Some wet their pants. Some ran off to find their mothers. Some did both.

One kid's hair caught on fire, and he fled into the woods, where he was caught by the double-headed Hemlock Hurdler. The next day, all we found were some bloody bones in the bushes and tuft of scorched hair on a raspberry thorn.

I was so good at telling stories that I was told to stop. But sometimes stories just happen.

A lot of stories still happen thanks to the Connecticut Storytelling Center (CSC). It was founded 40 years ago by Barbara Reed a professor at Connecticut College. For the last 20 years it's been under director Ann Shapiro, with an office at the college.

And then one day Little Mr. Coronavirus came to town.

Now the Center is uncentered. Everybody works from home.

But the storytelling goes on—or at least it's trying to. A big part of storytelling has always been the proximity of the storyteller and the audience. The audience needs to hear the voice, see the gestures, and sense each others' presence. The storyteller needs to read the audience and their eyes.

For the last 39 years, the Center has held an annual storytelling festival. It was mostly for teachers, librarians, and storytellers, an opportunity to do more than hear tales. They learned about the benefits of oral stories and how to use them to teach children.

The Center also sent a couple dozen storytellers to schools across the state, and not just for entertainment. Storytelling is more pedagogical than the kids ever suspect. Listening to a story involves several skills. Kids need to follow logic, chronology, and cause-and-effect. They need to remember. They need to visualize. They need to cooperate, to respect, to shut up and pay attention.

The typical classroom story isn't just a few minutes of narrative. It involves audience participation—the storyteller eliciting responses, calling for suggestions, checking on comprehension, holding attention by the scruff of its neck.

Every year some ten thousand Connecticut kids get to hear CSC storytellers at school. But now the kids are distanced. Everybody's wearing a mask. And nobody needs an outsider coming in to spew fairy tales and germs.

So how's storytelling supposed to work?

Good question. So far, no good answer.

The obvious but not-so-good answer: an internet conference. Kids in one place, the storyteller in a land far, far away. Participation is awkward. Eye contact is impossible. The rare opportunity for in-person communication is back on a screen like just about everything else these days.

Gathering around a computer screen just isn't the same as gathering around a lady dressed up like Mother Goose. It's uncomfortably like watching TV. Still, Ann Shapiro says it seems to be working—not perfectly. It's better than TV but not nearly as much fun as a small fire on the classroom floor.

Whence Your Honey

A lot of eastern Connecticut's honeybees come from the back end of a horse trailer.

It's a long story involving a long drive, a short horse trailer, and a medium-sized beekeeper, Stuart Woronecki, Ph.D., owner of Stonewall Apiary.

Three times in early spring, Woronecki gets out of bed well before dawn. The empty trailer's already hitched to his pick-up. He makes coffee and heads south, hoping to clear New York before rush hour.

He keeps driving, all the way to southern Georgia, stopping for little but coffee and gasoline. In a time of Covid, he doesn't even stop for food. He fuels himself from a cooler, steering with his left hand, eating with his right.

Seventeen hours later, he pulls into Claxton, a town with a train track running through it, two hardware stores right downtown, and a grocery with a sign offering S&H Green Stamps.

He eats. He downs a gin and tonic, maybe two. He sleeps the good sleep in a cheap motel.

Next morning he hauls his trailer over to Wilbanks Apiary. Wilbanks has close to 10,000 hives, but it produces no honey. What it produces is bees, and that's what Woronecki has come for.

He backs his trailer up to a building. The last thing Wilbanks needs at this time of year is a virus, so they won't let him out of his truck. They let him roll his window down three inches, but everybody stands back.

A crew of Mexicans with agricultural visas loads the trailer with 451 screened boxes, each with some 3,000 bees, all of them very concerned about the situation. Each box also has a queen isolated in a special cage. She's concerned, too. The multitude around her aren't her subjects. They'd kill her if they could.

The crew staples the boxes into rows like high-rise apartments. They're tight in there. Now it isn't a horse trailer. It's a bee trailer.

Woronecki heads north. The 6.3 million bees are worth a good $30,000, but not if they're dead. They have to be in New London County, 1,003 miles away, by morning. There's no time for breakdowns, no allowance for an accident, no room for error, no fooling around en route, and definitely no gin and tonics.

He grabs coffee at truck stops. He steers with his left hand, he eats with his right. He drives all day, he drives all night.

Bees generate a lot of heat. The trailer has electric fans to cool them at the southern end of the trip. But at the northern end, they might get too cold. Woronecki watches the road with one eye, a thermometer with the other. Thirty thousand dollars has to be kept just right.

God, cops, weather and dumb luck willing, he pulls into Stonewall Apiary before dawn. His day's about half done.

He's got a crew of native Americans to help him unload—family, friends, employees. They move the 6.3 million bees to an air conditioned trailer. It's sweaty, sticky work that involves a few stings from bees clinging to the outside of the box screens, terrified, confused and doomed.

In a couple of hours, more than a hundred beekeepers start to drive up. They stay in their vehicles. The crew, huffing behind home-made face masks made by the beekeeper's wife, loads the trunks and pick-ups.

A little after noon, Woronecki takes a phone over to the bee yard, sets up a video stream to show people how to install a package of bees. The process is a little complicated.

First, you remove the queen cage, a little pine box with a screen. Behold her beauty! She's long and tan and oh-so-lovely, a girl from Ipanema with six legs, diaphanous wings and a spermatheca ready to go.

She has to eat herself out of the situation, licking her way through a tunnel packed with sugar candy. Worker bees lick their way in. It takes a few days. By the time they meet, the worker bees will love the smell of her. She will be their queen.

He tucks the cage into an unpopulated hive. Then he thumps the box of bees on the ground to knock them into a chaotic pile. Then he pulls off the lid and dumps everybody into the hive.

And there they are: home sweet home. Welcome to Connecticut, ladies.

Late afternoon, Woronecki goes home. He eats. He downs a gin and tonic, maybe two. He sleeps the good sleep.

Leo Connellan, Plain Poet Laureate

Leo Connellan, Connecticut Poet Laureate from 1996 until his death 20 years ago this February, lived in Norwich and Sprague for the last two decades of his life. He was a man to be noticed when he lived and to be remembered for all he accomplished.

Connellan wasn't a mainstream poet out of an ivory tower. He was tidewater out of Maine. You could tell from his ratty sweater vests, his sore-hip shuffle, his perpetual disgruntlement, and his growl at any sign of injustice or disrespect for the shaggy side of life.

His life took a turn for the better in 1987, when he was named poet-in-residence for the Connecticut State University System. But he trusted good fortune about as much as Downeasters trust a sunny sky.

In 1996, life got even better when Connellan replaced state poet laureate James Merrill upon his death that year.

The two poets could not have been more opposite. Merrill was born into the fortune of the founder of the Merrill Lynch investment firm. He never held a job other than eight months in the army and a leisurely lifetime as a writer and poet. Merrill accepted the poet laureate position under the condition that it would require no public activities.

Connellan, on the other hand, was born to a small town attorney and postmaster in Rockport, on Maine's Penobscot Bay. His mother died when he was 7, leaving him torn and traumatized as he was raised by a step-mother.

His neighbors were the type of people who wrestled lobster pots, hauled fish from an ice-cold sea, or took a chainsaw to work.

Once old enough to be on his own, he thumbed and bummed his way across the country for a few years, sleeping in fields, alleys and church missions, taking any little job he could find, panhandling when he found none.

He was 32 before he landed a real job, married a girl named Nancy, and settled down in Clinton, Conn.

It was a good job for a while. He was a regional sales manager, peddling typewriter ribbons and carbon paper from New England to Baltimore. Needless to say, his days as such were numbered. Three years before retirement, in the 1970s, his company went broke, and his family sought cheaper rent in Norwich and then, even cheaper, in Sprague, where he lived in the Hanover Apartments complex until he suffered a lethal stroke in February 2001.

Poetry is not a poor man's profession. It's a job for the wealthy or those who land a professorship with a salary. Leo Connellan got out of bed at 3 o'clock each morning, seven days a week, to sit at a

169

typewriter and think, perhaps to write. A couple hours later he went off to sweep floors, substitute teach or do whatever else he could to support his family and his writing.

Despite his humble background, Connellan was not a humble man. He was proud of his accomplishments, which included more than a dozen books of poetry and several prestigious awards. But he felt he deserved more than what he got. He didn't like The New York Times calling him a poet for the "voiceless working class." He considered himself a poet for everyone.

So he was a bit bitter about his lot in life. He treasured his hard-scrabble background, but he sensed an injustice at how hard he had to work while other poets hobnobbed in higher social circles.

A conversation with Connellan could quickly range across a spectrum from gruff righteousness to warm concern. He suffered the curse of the Irish but also their gift of gab and poesy.

As one friend said at his funeral at St. Patrick's Cathedral in Norwich, "Sometimes it was impossible to love Leo, and at the same time, it wasn't possible not to."

Connellan took his laureateship seriously. He went to elementary and high schools all over the state to plant the seeds of future poetry. He dispelled any notions that poetry was for the hoity-toity. He taught that the raw material of poetry was in the homes and streets and workplaces where plain people lead plain and beautiful lives.

It should be no surprise that such a poet found a home on the hardscrabble side of Connecticut.

The Art of Horror

O h, the horror! The horror!

Isn't there enough of it in the world?

Apparently not—not around here, anyway. Zombies are scarce. Mummies stick to their sarcophagi. Pythons aren't really a problem. If Satan's around, at least he's decent enough to wear a hat and keep his tail tucked in.

If you really want horror around here, you need to either do it yourself or pay to have it done.

The DIY approach is just going to get you in trouble, and it isn't nearly as much fun as the paid-for pandemonium at The Dark Manor in Versailles.

Let us pause for a moment of etymological reflection.

First of all, "Versailles," pronounced just the way it looks, isn't in France, where it is grotesquely mispronounced. It's the village in Sprague where the Vers Woolen Mill was bought by the Sayles family in 1871, when it became the Vers-Sayles Mill.

Second of all, "pandemonium" is derived from the Greek "pan," meaning "all," and "daimon," meaning "demon." And that's what people have been experiencing at the Dark Manor for the last 16 years.

The Dark Manor has all the demons the horror-starved need.

A cackling "mistress" welcomes the doomed. She warns them about the one truly deadly demon that lurks in the hellscape they are about to tour. They won't even see it. It's just 100 nanometers from head to toe, the coronavirus demon, lying in ambush on any given surface. The mistress warns the imminently terrified not to touch anything, and she assures that no one will touch them...at least no one alive.

So sanitize and abandon all hope, ye who enter there.

Once welcomed, the brave enter an infernal labyrinth of hair-raising distress. Animatronic monsters lurch up from nowhere. Windows snap open and zombies screech point-blank into the ear. A mutilated cadaver turns its head to greet you. A real, live predator warms up a real, live chainsaw.

And the clowns...

"Clown Town is the most terrifying," says Jonni Illinger, who lives in Hanover, on the other side of Sprague. "This is where we get the most wet pants."

Jonni's one of the 28 actors who do their best to tap bladders and purge intestines large and small. This year she's a Plague Doctor, scarier than a corpse of festering buboes. Her job is to enforce social distancing in that most unsociable place. Masks are mandatory. Infractions are punishable by death.

Other job titles: Chain Saw Guy, Grass Man, Michael Meyers, Shovel Girl, Creepy Nurse/Skilsaw operator, Drop-Down Guy...

The actors are trained for emergencies. They have fire extinguishers. They know what to do when a guest freaks out. They know how to mop up.

The dim path of the labyrinth winds through a dismal swamp, a murderous mining camp, a catacomb of bones, a graveyard, a Blood Shed, a surgery room, a conclave of spiders the size of schnauzers.

Screams, screeches, roars and cackles, distant and near, unsettle the air. Webs dangle. Slimy fingers beckon. Germicidal fog slithers along the ground.

Among Jonni's projects this year is to re-dress an animatronic alien as a giant praying mantis.

"This is not for children," Jonni warns. "I wouldn't let a kid under 13 go in there. No [freakin'] way."

The Dark Manor is the twisted brainchild of Rick Peirce. Peirce had never been especially interested in the horror industry, or even aware of it, until about 20 years ago. He was at a costume trade show when he started talking with a vendor of horror products.

By the end of the conversation, he knew he could make a business of a haunted house.

He started on Long Island, where people lined for three hours to get in. Then he bought an old brick Masonic Temple in Versailles. Over the years it became more and more sophisticated.

"You can't just build a place like this," he says. "It takes 15 years."

Fifteen years and a lot of creativity. Each year he and Jonni and other associates accumulate more and more artifacts of ghastliness. Today they have dozens of animatronic devices, extraordinary costumes, scores of skeletons, guts galore, ghouls out the kazoo.

As they brew up each year's new program, they find stuff they forgot they had, stuff not found in the average place of business—a bag of bats, a head with a knife in it, a box of bloody feet, a bin labeled simply "Hands."

They are the home decorators of Hell. They take the real and make it unreal, but as realistic as possible.

"It's art," Peirce says. "Horror is art."

Boy meets Girl, East meets West, Front meets Back

Understanding an artist's mind isn't easy. And it shouldn't be. We look to artists to think the unthought, see the unseen, and shine a light in places we didn't know were dark.

Or, as Confucius put it, "Everything has its beauty, but not everyone sees it."

Case in point: the Patnodes.

You may know of Mark Patnode. For many years he's been painting warm, shimmering images of buildings in New London and landscapes along the Connecticut coast. His scenes are within a hundred feet of sea level.

Last year, Mark married Zhai Yujuan, an artist from a Himalayan region twice the altitude of Denver. No mysterious artistic musing behind that decision. Altitude had nothing to do with it. She's as sweet and pleasant as the month of June, the month when spring meets summer, the basis of her adopted name, Juner. Mark could not resist. He didn't even try.

Now Mark and Juner share an apartment on Granite St., a studio on Washington St., and a vision which, like beauty itself, transcends place.

He paints on canvas, oils of classically Western scenes—brick buildings, sea marshes, meadows edged by maple and oak.

She paints on rice paper and silk, watercolors of distinctly Eastern beauty—flowers, butterflies, blossomed branches, the occasional portrait.

Boy meets girl. East meets West. Spring meets summer, and sea level meets altitude. Contrary to the conflicts rending the world, these opposites are coming together in a mutual vision of beauty.

The artists have an idea. It involves beauty meeting philosophy.

As part of his training back in art school, Mark drew nudes. He had to. It was required. It wasn't a bad way to spend an academic afternoon, certainly better than, say, cramming for an exam in organic chemistry.

Still, his artistic muse led him into landscapes and urban scenes. But recently he's had nudes in mind again. He's thinking about a side of nudes rarely depicted—their backs, a Confucian beauty that not everyone sees.

Mark's idea became Juner's idea, a shared idea for a shared project. They are going to draw, paint, and possibly photograph the backs of nudes. They want to demonstrate, through artistic interpretation, how the Western eye and the Eastern eye interpret the same conceptual subject.

The subjects—the models— will be from different parts of the world. For this project to come together, the artists will need backs from not only the West and the East but from the Northern and Southern hemispheres. They want East and West to meet North and South.

Can these disparate regions and cultures, these opposites, get along in a world cleaved by passionate differences?

Juner and Mark (and Confucius) think so. They think they can take the unseen side of people, the side without a face, the side free from prejudice and attitude—their backs—and make those backs the side people see. Through the minds and visions of two artists, backs become fronts.

Boy meets girl. East meets West. North meets South. Front meets back. See?

It takes the mind of an artist—or in this case, two artists—to unify such ideas and render them as visual images. The opposites meet in beauty rather than conflict, in light where it might otherwise be dark.

"Back to Front" is the working title of the Patnode project. What forms it will take, how it will unfold, what it will look like, they do not yet know. But they have begun. They will see where their art takes them. That's how art works. It's a light exploring the dark. It's the search for the beauty in everything. It's bringing everything together in beauty, because in beauty, everything gets along.

How It Went

Among the many weird things that happen in New London, the annual Mayfly plays rank among the most stellar. On a Friday evening in the dead of winter, six playwrights are handed assignments. Each has to write a play and hand it in by morning. They have 12 hours to crank out the impossible.

No cheating! The assignments include certain props, themes, and lines that must be included. The plays must be written for a certain number of characters. Until that Friday evening, only the producer knows these details.

The next morning, six troupes are handed the plays. The have but 12 hours to prepare. Dress rehearsals start at 5:00 that afternoon. The performances start at 8:00.

What could possibly go wrong? Well, plenty.

Trouble is, the show must go on. Neither snow nor rain nor heat nor gloom nor a fire upstairs shall stay these thespians from their hour upon the stage.

That's what happened last year—a fire upstairs. And that was just the last of several things that went wrong. The impossible really was impossible. But they did it anyway.

At the center of the 24 hours of rolling catastrophe was producer Kato McNickle. Kato's credentials defy credence. She writes plays, directs plays, produces plays, edits plays, and plays in plays. She's done the world-famous O'Neill Theater in Waterford. She's won awards.

Under pressure, she's cool as a cuke. She prepares with the acumen of a CEO, and she leads with military discipline. She's an optimist who knows that everything's going to go wrong, so she prepares like a pessimist in a foxhole. She has six rehearsal areas ready, plus a couple of back-ups just in case. She has an extra writer in case one of the others gets sick or something. She has a few extra actors ready to go. She has extra props. She has garbage bags for the rehearsal trash. She has extra garbage bags. She has solutions all set before the problems even think about popping up.

When the Friday evening in the dead of winter comes around, she's ready. She becomes a clock with an iron fist in a padded oven mitt. Forty-eight people know what to do and where to be at any given moment in the next 24 hours. No exceptions. No excuses. She tells them what must be done, but she's nice about it. Gentle. She wants Mayfly to happen, but nobody gets hurt.

Last year, for the 12th annual Mayfly, a certain writer came in from New York to write one of the plays. She was prone to social anxiety, so the last thing she needed was a laptop that wouldn't boot.

But that's what she had, and the only solution was back in New York. A show can't go on if it doesn't get written, so Kato dispatched a techie. But the case was beyond first aid, so Kato came up with a laptop, and the writer got to work.

Next morning, the writers emailed their plays to Kato. Five were on time, but for some reason, one of them caused Kato's computer to crash. It crashed and crashed and crashed. The actors were waiting, sweating in the dead of winter. They were going to be on stage in 12 hours. It was down to 11 hours before a convoluted internet process got the file open and the play printed.

The sixth writer finished his play, shot it off by email, turned off his phone and, exhausted from his all-nighter, hit the hay. He'd forgotten that he'd turned off his wifi so nobody could bother him. The email sat idling in his outbox while his eager actors stewed. His phone off, he couldn't be roused. Somebody had to go find his hotel room and pound on his door until he woke up. It took a while. He was tired.

By 5:00, everyone convened for dress rehearsal at the ballroom of the Crocker House, where Eugene O'Neill himself once wet his whistle. The doors were to open in two hours. Five o'clock was also the hour that water started dripping from the ceiling. Then it started gushing. Then the ceiling started falling in. Then the fire trucks arrived. The Crocker was on fire.

The troupes withdrew and regrouped at the Hygienic Gallery, the organizer of the event. Kato was cool. She knew something like this was going to happen. She quickly calculated three options: They could say to hell with it and go have dinner. They could go find some little space somewhere and put on the performance just for themselves. Or by hook or crook they can present the plays to the public.

Things don't happen when people say to hell with it, and a show isn't really going on if it's in somebody's garage. The show must go on...but where? It was almost 6:00...

Halfway between the Crocker and the Hygienic, conveniently across the street from the Dutch Tavern, was a wide-open space the Democratic Party was using as headquarters. Because this was in New London and not some normal town, it took just one phone call to get permission and a key. The doors opened to the public by 8:00, and the show went on.

The Mayfly plays will take place again this year smack-dab in the middle of the winter—February 1. According to plan, it will happen at the Crocker House. It will be the 13th performance. What could possibly go wrong? Kato knows, and she's ready.

Asphalt Art at the Intersection of Green, Golden, and Tears

If you're in downtown New London much, you've probably seen it. It's a big, circular work of art filling the intersection of Golden and Green.

If you were walking, you may have stopped and given it some thought—the pizzaesque slices of yellow and red, the angular, Escheresque spirals of turquoise and ultramarine.

If you were driving, you probably rolled right over it with a sense of either obliviousness or guilt.

New London is a town of murals—whales, caryatids, guitars, people, scenes—art that needs the great outdoors, art that can't be contained.

But all murals are on walls. This intriguing round masterpiece surrounding a manhole cover just down the street from the Dutch Tavern isbn't a mural. It's more of a mandala.

The words painted along the eastern rim explain it a bit. They say, "In Memory of Chris Nelson."

That also explains why it's known as the Nelson Mandala.

A plaque on a nearby wall preserves more information.

Chris Nelson was a man who loved New London. In fact, he loved cities. He believed in cities, believed they could be warm, human, inviting and enriching.

No wonder he left New York City and settled here. New York has plenty to offer, but it doesn't have friends who meet once a year to repaint pavement in your memory.

Chris was a founding member of the Green Party in New London. He epitomized the Green philosophy of society working together to make life better for everyone. His insightful language—"Chrisisms"—still grace the party bylaws.

He understood what makes New London tick—the art, music, ideas, ideals, idealisms, idiosyncrasies, the nitty-gritty of artisanship and the sense of a nearby sea.

Like a lot of people in New London, he was well educated but found peace in a blue collar profession. He majored in political philosophy at Yale but earned his living as a shipwright. He was one of few people in the world who could caulk the old-fashioned way.

In a sense, Chris lived political philosophy. If he wasn't building a boat, refurbishing a historical building on Green St. or thrashing his way to victory on a basketball court, he was trying to make New London a better city. He pushed for establishing Riverside Park. He helped organize Earth Day. In ways too quiet for most people to notice, he advocated innovative changes for the better. If he wasn't advocating at town hall, he was opining at the Dutch.

He served on the city's planning & zoning commission,

bringing to it a political philosophy that was informed and insightful, somehow both realistic and idealistic. He warned about a city being planned and zoned to death. He wanted to see neighborhoods develop organically into functional clusters of business and residence.

I knew Chris from the anti-war efforts of a few—too few—citizens who objected to the invasion of Iraq. He struck me as one of the most intelligent and insightful people I have ever met. Every conversation with him was interesting. I always came away with raised awareness.

Everyone else felt the same about him. And that's why once a year, early on a Sunday in the spring, a bunch of his friends and family come together at the intersection of Green and Golden to repaint the mandala in memoriam. They mix traffic paint just right. They sweep off dirt and scrub off tread marks. They try to keep their lines straight. They hold themselves to a high standard. Then they repair to the Dutch to recover and recall.

Chris held himself to a high standard, too. Everyone admired his intelligence and idealism and thought his flaws insignificant, even beautiful. But he was brutally critical of himself. Too critical. He loved his city but not himself. He died in June of 2013. He was 43.

Pox Americana

What To Do in Times of Uncertain Inevitability

Covid-19 won't kill me, but the uncertainty sure might. I'm not afraid of the germs. I've dealt with germs before.

And I'm not afraid of what might happen. I've dealt with might-happens before. So far, what was going to happen happened. And then something else happened. Not much is certain in this new world we're in, but one thing's for sure: something's going to happen.

What worries me is having to make decisions and help other people make decisions when none of us really knows what will happen or even what just might happen. We're all in front of the big slot machine of life in a time of plague. We don't know what will happen if we pull the handle, what will happen if we don't. Something is inevitable, yet everything is uncertain.

My wife and I have a guest house we rent out on AirBnB. Our current guests are refugees out of New York who got out just in time. But they reserved only a month. They're trying to run two small but international businesses over cell phones at the woodsier end of

Connecticut. I don't know exactly what they do, but I think it involves perfumes from France, manufacturing in China, and clients in New York. Nobody in any of those places knows what's happening now, let alone next week.

Then a mother and a four-year-old—more refugees from New York—want to rent the place next month. Before accepting, I offer to let the current people extend their stay. They don't know what to do. Going home seems pointless. A quarantined apartment in the desert of New York is no closer to Paris, China, or a Manhattan storefront than a guest house in the woods. The world is now as close as a cell phone pressed to the ear and as far as a space probe crackling in from Neptune.

The mother and child could come in June, but another guest is scheduled for the middle of that month. He's coming from South Carolina to build a church in Jewett City along with 150 other people. Is this church urgent enough to have 150 Baptists sneezing on each other for a week? It's hard to say, and it's not his decision. He has to wait. I have to wait. The mother and child have to wait. God has to wait.

What I needed to do was manhandle some firewood. My wood yard looked like a muddy battlefield where the trees had lost bad. Limbs and logs had been lying there for half the winter. I didn't care that it was raining. I couldn't solve the Covid problem, and I couldn't tell what might happen in a week or a month, but I could pick up a hunk of wood and throw it where it had to go. If it needed splitting, I heaved it into the to-split pile. If it didn't, I flipped it over to the to-stack pile. If it still needed to get sawed up, I left it where it was.

Moving firewood around is so simple, all brute tactility, every move obvious, every result predictable. No big decisions, no mistakes possible. Tossing my logs hither and yon, soft rain dripping off my hat, gloves slimy with wet lichen, I thought about the more difficult triages happening in New York. People had to decide if a cough is just a cough. Dispatch had to decide where to send the ambulance. Some people were getting into hospitals; some were getting turned away at the door. Some got respirators; some didn't. Every decision was big, and they were all mistakes. Every possible decision was a mistake.

I thought about what's certain. This, too, shall pass always holds true, but what happens after that? We were certain that this was inevitable, but only in retrospect. Same goes for the inevitable "I told you so." I stood there in the soft rain, thinking about hard rain, wondering about uncertainty and inevitability and which I would pick if I had the option to decide.

Philosophy for a Time of Peril

Rubem Alves was a theologian, philosopher, and psychoanalyst who lived in the mountains of Brazil but seemed to write for people on the coast of Connecticut. His warm and avuncular thoughts transcended continents and cultures to touch any human heart.

Rubem saw the meaning of life in a kernel of popcorn. He saw connections between gardening and politics, pain and poetry, soup and sex. He opined on toys with batteries. He saw beauty in the most mundane. He offered insights to the soul.

"Candles cry when they illuminate," he wrote. "Their tears, born of fire, spill over and run down their body. They cry because they know that, to shine, they must die."

Once you've read that, you can never see candles the same again.

But then it's your birthday, and you think about this:

"The custom of blowing out birthday candles is morbid. A candle should never be blown out. There's always the danger that the gods won't understand what we're asking for when we extinguish the flame, a symbol of life."

He can't even make popcorn without getting all metaphysical about it. Those little kernels seem so hard and inedible, so useless, so inferior to the sweet yellow nuggets of silver queen on a cob. But when you heat them up—give them a trial by fire—most of them blossom into something beautiful. The kernels, he imagines, aren't really happy about being boiled in oil, but that's what they need to truly become soft and beautiful, to be what they were meant to be.

And life's like that, isn't it? Great transformations happen under the force of fire. Those who refuse to change under the pain of heat, the kernels that refuse to pop, remain hard and unfulfilled.

Suffering, he says, prepares the soul for a vision of something new. Pain turns into poetry, an object of communion, a sacrament. The vocation of poets: "to put words in places where the pain is too acute."

And of all the vocations, he says, "politics is the most noble." He cites an ancient Hebrew to define politics as "the art of gardening applied to public things."

But are all politicians noble? Most certainly not. Because vocation is one thing, profession another. In a vocation, one finds happiness in the act itself. In a profession, the pleasure is only in the gain derived, most commonly a pile of moolah. Of all the professions, he says, "professional politics is the most vile."

He implies that professional politicians (and lousy gardeners) come from childhoods in dumbed-down houses (all decor, no books) cursed with dumbed-down toys:

"Toys that work with only the push of a button to make something happen are dumbed-down objects—push the button, the doll sings; push the other button, the doll pees; push a button, the car goes. They don't make us think. As soon as a girl decides to do surgery on a doll to see how the magic happens—at that moment she starts getting smart."

Would you be surprised to know that Rubem Alves has a bookshelf in his bathroom? That explains how he cites Nietzsche, Freud, Neruda, Auden, Drummond, Eliot, Pessoa, Shakespeare, Hesse, Borges, Bachelard, Barthes, Goethe, Jesus, Peter Pan, Snow White, Cinderella, Scheherazade. He peers into the depths of Dali, Escher, Vermeer, Rodin, Bach, and the Tao.

He appreciates a weed, a cow flop, a bowl of soup, ipé petals on a sidewalk, a bem-te-vi bird, trees groaning with pleasure as they rub against each other.

What is a love letter, he asks, but "a paper that connects two lonelinesses." What is love "but a desire to eat and be eaten"? What is a laugh but "an ejaculation of joy" that reveals a secret of the soul? What is the soul but "a maze of caverns lit by a light that infiltrates through narrow cracks, caverns that grow ever deeper and darker"?

He has so much to say about the soul. Almost every page mentions it. The soul does not like to march, he says; it's a ballerina who likes to dance. It's a song being played. It is lightness within the body's weight, a butterfly within a corporeal cocoon. Its wings are called courage. At its deepest place, it's a scene of happiness. It craves the noble things above: truth, beauty, and the good.

Rubem Alves thrust such thoughts in the face of a military dictatorship that put power and piles of moolah above life, art, love, and the soul. Alas, he did not live to enlighten us in a time of plague and planetary meltdown. His soul emerged from its cocoon in 2014 and left us here to figure stuff out on our own.

Our Resurrection

Consider the caterpillar: wooly, ruddy, creeping at the pace of an old man with a cane. It knows it has to die. It wants to die. It finds a snug spot and builds itself a shroud out of its own body. It goes into deep sleep—as far as a caterpillar can tell, an eternal sleep.

And pretty soon, at just the right time, a butterfly, as light as a soul, in all the beauty due youth, breaks out of the cocoon, dusts itself off, and flutters into the sunlight.

I confess I swiped that lovely metaphor of transformation and resurrection from Brazilian philosopher and theologian Rubem Alves. He used it to make the point that, for something to be born, something else must die. That's what change is.

He wasn't thinking about pandemics, but the principle applies.

The virus and the isolation will bring about a lot of change. A way of life—actually, millions of ways of life—will die. New ways of living will be reborn from the old ways. We will transform. We will become something that we are not now.

Things work out well for the caterpillar. It becomes something beautiful. No longer crawling, it flies.

But does that apply to people?

Will we accomplish the same upward transformation when we emerge from our quarantine cocoons? Will we continue to be an empathetic society, people as concerned about infecting as getting infected? Will we find new strength as we rebuild? Will we fly?

More specifically, will we learn we can work from home, maybe even work fewer days? Will we start new kinds of businesses? Will we learn how to help schools by extending education to the home? Will we be more careful about what we believe? Will our values be a little different? Will we appreciate the banal—the endless bounty of store shelves, the walk in fresh air, the chummy get-togethers, children running around in the sun like inebriated butterflies?

Or will be go back down to the dirt of contention, self-interest, false logic, and faith in the fake?

In the Tarot deck there is a card called The Tower. It's a powerful Higher Arcana card that depicts a forbidding stone tower as it is hit by lightning. Flames lick from the windows and people tumble into a dark and stormy night.

But the tower itself does not fall. Only its façade cracks and flakes away. The death of the façade reveals an inner truth, an insight into reality, exposure of what was hidden, the disappearance of illusion. It's a good card to get in a reading, but not without trepidation for those who cling to the fraudulent façade of appearance.

Another Higher Arcana card, Death, also presents a deceptive image, a skeleton in dark armor on a pale horse. But the card does not refer to a tragic end. It predicts a radical, sweeping change, a rising to a higher level of existence, a better understanding of the world. The card means to say that there is no end; there is only change—the death of one thing, the birth of another.

The pain and in some cases true tragedy of the pandemic will force us to change. We will learn what we can live without. We'll treasure toilet paper over caviar. We'll have a better understanding of what's important. We'll appreciate people and public spaces. We're already bursting with thanks for the medical professionals, for the people who stock the shelves, for the truck drivers, for the under-paid who are suddenly essential—in a certain sense butterflies we'd never noticed.

And when this is over, we'll be thankful for friends and strangers just because they're among us. We'll be thankful for the waitress, the librarian, the teacher, the wooly, ruddy old man with a cane smiling at the little butterflies running around in the sun.

Wake Up, America!

Buried alive in a box? You've got a real problem and not much time to solve it. If you've been embalmed, of course, your problems are over. You are more than dead. Not even a worm would eat you. You're going to be more than dead for a long, long time.

But if you should find yourself in the situation of awakening in a coffin, first ask yourself how you know you're in a coffin and not just some dark, horizontal refrigerator box. Do you remember being at a party where a lot of tequila was involved? Do you remember dying? If so, odds are you aren't in a coffin. You're in bed and you're asleep and having a bad dream. Try waking up.

If waking up doesn't work, try going to sleep. That will minimize your consumption of oxygen. You'll live longer. And then die. Like everybody else. Just be glad nobody pumped formaldehyde into your veins. Rest in peace.

But you may be too excited to fall asleep. Who could blame you? It's like your first day on a new job. You're confused. You're nervous. You want to do things right, but you haven't received proper training. They've thrown you into a new situation, and you've hit the ground running. Or, in this case, lying down.

Relax. You've got enough oxygen for a couple of hours. You'll wake up in time. Because really, you're just dreaming this.

With a little luck you'll dream you were buried with your cell phone. This is far more likely than being buried alive. Of course it's also likely your battery's dead. (That's why they buried it with you! Ha, ha—just a little coffin humor. Have yourself a last chuckle.)

Of course you may have been fortunate enough to have received a green burial. A green burial is just what it sounds like: they paint you green and pack you in four-leaf clover with a bottle of Irish whiskey under your arm to ease your transition to eternity.

Not really. A green burial is an organic burial. No embalming. No concrete vault. No polyester suit. No plastic buttons. No pocket change. If you're in a casket, it's plain vanilla pine or cardboard—no paint, no varnish, no liner, no bells, no whistles, no frills.

Also no cell phone, not unless it's biodegradable.

But maybe they forgot it was in your pocket, and the battery is no deader than you, and you aren't in a concrete vault six feet under, just four feet under and no vault, and in an organic cardboard casket in a cemetery in the shadow of a cell tower. Try calling 9-1-1, see if they believe you. (They won't. And anyway, what are you going to give them for an address?)

Next try calling the most dependable person you know who owns a shovel or, better yet, a backhoe. Tap your head gently on the bottom of the coffin, and then harder and harder as you listen to the detailed instructions on how to leave a message. Make sure you mention that you're leaving the message AFTER the funeral.

Try texting. Text your entire list of contacts. And pray—pray that you aren't doing this in your sleep. Which you probably are. And everyone you know is going to get the message. They're going to wonder why they weren't invited to the funeral.

But they'll figure it out. And they will never let you forget. And for the rest of your life, you're going to wish you were dead. And someday you will be—hopefully before you're buried. But this time, be smart. Get buried green.

Maybe It's Just Me

Road Signs

I take long walks in the morning, a mile or two at least, sometimes three or four. It's a peaceful walk at dawn down rural roads straying between New London and Windham counties. Not one to waste time mono-tasking, I pick up litter along the way. I keep almost ten miles of road clean.

I find all kinds of stuff. Mostly it's beer cans, snack bags, fast-food containers, little nip bottles, and assorted rags of styrofoam. Like everything else in the universe, each item is a sign of something. Most of the signs indicate that a lot of people are driving around drunk, and that Connecticut still has a substantive population of people who weren't raised very well.

Now and then I find a gem—not something worth money but, to me, worth thought, little mysteries of litter, signs pointing into the unknown and inexplicable. You won't see these signs if you're driving by, and you sure won't find them on the internet. You need to walk, and you need to poke around where other people don't poke.

One bright morning I saw a dull green glint under dead leaves. It was a 7-Up bottle, an old one with the label printed right on the glass. It was dirty but cleaned up real nice. Not a scratch on it. I gave it to the historical society. They did some research and learned it had been made in 1948.

Now how did that happen—a bottle lying within six feet of a road for 72 years? Or had someone recently driven by in a Studebaker and finally finished off the last of a very flat soda and chucked the bottle out the window?

I was wondering about that when I started finding golf balls, one or two a day, miles apart, on various roads. Each ball was unique, either a brand unlike the others or bearing the name of a conference or tournament. Some were lime green, some florescent pink. Never the same ball twice.

This was a sign of what? Someone disposing of a golf ball collection by tossing one or two a day out a car window? If you have an explanation, please contact me. Likewise, if you'd like a golf ball collection, I have more than a hundred and no particular interest in golf.

Nor do I have any particular interest in possums, but a small one lying in the road caught my attention. I was driving at the time. Like most possums, it was dead. But not flat. It lay curled up like a fetus, its tiny front paws crossed just below its chin. Playing possum? I doubted it, but in a moment of pointless, posthumous mercy, I swerved around it.

The next morning, I walked past that same spot. The possum now lay in a grassy area beside the road, still unscathed. Someone had actually stopped and moved the poor little thing to a safer place. I was comforted to find a sign of a person like that. Some throw their fast-food trash out the window. Some drive around drunk. And some will stop to do a dead possum a favor.

Some are a little too careless with their mail. I found a damp and wrinkled letter from the Bureau of Child Support Enforcement addressed to a certain William. William had an outstanding balance of $49,657.01 in unpaid child support. The child, a girl, did not have William's last name. William's last name just happened to be the same as the name on a mailbox just up the road. The mailbox also bore, rather boldly, the title of a position in our state criminal justice system—a sign of hypocrisy and pride.

Being a person of felonious instinct, I immediately sensed the potential for extortion. But I restrained myself. The signs weren't all pointing in the same direction. The car in the driveway was a Prius with a Hillary bumpersticker. Was William a feminist dead-beat dad with an environmental conscience? It didn't make sense. (Then again, neither did the 7-Up bottle, the golf balls, or the possum.)

Months later I found a large damp and wrinkled envelope addressed to a woman with William's last name. The address was a State office in Hartford. She, it seemed, was the person with liberal inclinations and a job in law enforcement. And William was, in all likelihood—I'm just guessing here—divorced.

In an unrelated discovery a few miles away, I found another sign of familial distress. It was a travel mug in perfect condition. It had just one word on it: Mom.

How sad is that? Sadder than a dead possum. Sadder than abandoned golf balls or a cold and lonely old 7-Up bottle. Sadder than drunk litterbugs. Almost as sad as a dead-beat dad. So many signs of sadness, and no one sees them but me.

Peace and People Given a Chance

I bought something that wasn't made in China!

Dumb luck on my part. I hadn't given any thought to where it was made. But I'm always glad to throw my business to an underdog. It was a table, and the underdog was Vietnam.

Vietnam. I came of age when it wasn't a country, it was a war. It was flaming controversy. It was demonstrations that turned into riots, liberation that turned into My Lai, lies that turned into denials. It was an anti-war war. It was napalm, B-52s, Hueys, Agent Orange, the draft and daily death tolls—theirs and ours—reported on TV like the score of a game

But it was a perverse game with an inverted score. The one with the most points was losing.

The table arrived in a heavy flat box on a sunny spring day. It was an outdoor table, slats of acacia with steel legs and supports, several bags of assembly hardware, great gobs of protective packaging, and a tiny red sticker that said in tiny white letters, "Made in Vietnam."

In a gesture of undeserved generosity and understanding, the manufacturer had included one extra of each bolt, screw and washer, even an extra allen wrench. The assembly instructions were also generously redundant, with illustrations and clear explanations in—significantly—English.

Bygones, it seemed, have become bygones. We won the body count but failed to win the war. The communists prevailed. We perpetuated unimaginable horrors on the Vietnamese people, but the war machine and untold billions of dollars failed to solve the problem.

More than 2,400 years before the fake battle of the Gulf of Tonkin, Sun Tzu, master of war, warned us. He said, "The greatest victory is that which requires no battle."

He was right. As it turned out, we solved the problem not by battle but by absence. We simply left.

The proof is in my table. Its production and shipment to our western shore had to involve wages, laws, bilateral trade agreements, investment, banks, credit, currency exchange, international payments, contracts, insurance, negotiation, lawyers, promises, profit and a whole lot of styrofoam. The workers who made the table and packaged it with such care may well have taken their wages to McDonald's for a Happy Meal.

Add it all up and it looks a lot like capitalism. Or call it business. Or, in my case, a table. It all worked so smoothly. For a reasonable price, no blood, no sweat, no tears, there it was at my door on a sunny spring day. All the B-52s in the world could not have produced a better table or made the process any smoother.

And I must say, it's a very nice table. Handsome. Sturdy. Impervious to rain. The specs say it will seat six and hold 550 pounds of food.

I'm so glad the strife of the past has been resolved with some goodwill, a few jobs and a table where half a dozen people can break a quarter ton of bread. Why didn't we think of that 50 years ago? A job, a decent wage, some junk food and a Coke...so much more persuasive than napalm.

I did not go to Vietnam, neither the country nor the war. Again, just dumb luck. The very same day I became eligible for the draft, rated 1-A like the beef of a Big Mac, the secretary of defense came on TV and announced the end of military conscription.

The sigh of relief could be heard from my mother's lips to the jungles of southeast Asia. Those who knew me then knew I was not one to be entrusted with a machine gun, much less under hot and humid conditions. I would have only made a bad situation worse.

Left to its own devices, Vietnam has learned to do business. It mixes a little socialism, a little capitalism, a little diktat, and a little free enterprise. It makes its own styrofoam, and it stays out of wars.

Funny how things work out when you give peace a chance.

Saving the World One Move at a Time

I bought a nice chess set a few years ago, an antique from the 19th century. It was beautiful: maple pieces in classic Staunton form, the white pieces actually tan from time and thousands of moves.

Just one problem: someone had absconded with the white king.

It was actually a good problem. The critically defective set didn't cost much more than something plastic out of China.

I asked a local woodworker if he could make me a king. I gave him the black king and asked him to make one just like it. He did a pretty good job, even painting it black like the one he copied.

I repainted the king to a hue close to tan. The set served me well until a puppy and a one-year-old came along. A white rook disappeared, either chewed to unidentifiable splinters or poked into the kind of place that only a toddler can find.

I cannibalized another chess set, using its castle to substitute for the one that had disappeared. But it's just pine or fir, light-weight, not up to the work of a rook. It hunkers like a peasant favela next door to the regal ranks of its maple compatriots.

A chess board is a vicious place. All the pieces are people, save the rooks, which are homes with a capacity to wander. The opposing peoples slaughter each other. They sacrifice others for a greater cause. And the pawns, the peons, weak, multitudinous afterthoughts, have to be dealt with – blocked or taken – lest they advance too far and become whoever they want to be.

Jorge Luis Borges characterized this MacBethesque intrigue in a poem titled "Chess":

> *Frail king, angling bishop, bloody-minded*
> *queen, single-minded rook, cunning pawn,*
> *on the path of black and white,*
> *seek out and wage their armed battle...*

At a trade show for gifts or something I came upon a booth that offered chess sets with pieces representing scores of classic conflicts: Romans vs. Egyptians, Redcoats vs. Revolutionaries, Red Sox vs. Yankees, Russians vs. Americans, Democrats vs. Republicans, dogs vs. cats, ogres vs. trolls, Star Wars Imperials vs. Rebels, bourgeois bankers vs. proletarian slobs.

But I'm a man without gambit. I can't muster aggression without due cause. A friend and I used to play a cooperative version of the game. We'd explain each of our moves so that the other would know our purpose and plan. If one of us was thinking three moves ahead, we revealed those moves. Thus we took the world's most logical game and purified it of the contaminant of surprise.

Borges wrote another poem that likened two proletarian players to people who pet sleeping animals, plant gardens, search for meaning in etymology, and pause to appreciate the existence of music. "These people," he wrote, "without knowing it, are saving the world."

My brother-in-law did his bit to save the world by putting a soapstone chess set at the bottom of a swimming pool. He and another slacker took turns diving down to move a piece, then come up to report the move. It helped them develop memory. He developed the ability to play five games at once without seeing the boards. But he was never good at anything else in life, other than holding his breath. He wielded an excess of logic in an illogical world.

The puppy has moved on to a happier place (Uncasville), and the toddler, forgiven for his sin, is about to turn six. I'm teaching him to play the game. With our reconstructed queen and foreign rook, we grapple with the concepts of protection, sacrifice, and thinking ahead. I can still beat him every time, but he doesn't seem to mind. Each time I corner his king, he utters a thoughtful "Oh" of discovery and understanding, and the world has been saved once again.

When Incompetence Counts

I think my résumé needs rebranding.

I've been taking the wrong approach, hawking my degrees and experience, my accomplishments and competencies, all the glories that are my professional self. They've resulted in zilch.

I haven't even made it to an interview. Which is probably good because it would have gone something like this:

"So, Mr. Cheney, we notice a little gap in your employment between 1985 and ... the present?"

"Yes, I took a little time off to find myself."

"Does that explain this banana farm in Brazil?"

"It seemed like a good idea at the time..."

All too recently I've discovered the professional niche I should be wiggling into. I see a huge need out there, and no one is applying for the many jobs. I think I'm going to become a professional idiot.

It's technology that has opened this new field. By definition, high tech is dominated by highly competent people. They are competent beyond the reach of my imagination.

The unrecognized corollary is that I am incompetent beyond their imagination.

And I'm not alone. There are millions of us: people who have mastered the operation of on-off switches but can't find much meaning in instructions stripped down to an absolute minimum of information.

I'm looking at you, Error 404. And your shady accomplice over there, Error 500. And wipe that smirk off your face, little mister Syntax Error.

Information technology engineers can deal with that. English majors can't. Old English majors are even worse off. And their grandmothers might as well stick to their knitting.

IT engineers are too competent to understand the transcendental mystery of a "Printer Not Connected" message when any idiot can see that a printer is indeed connected.

That's where the Professional Idiot comes in. The PI knows how to not understand. Dizzying confusion is the PI's primary skill. A good PI can be an endless resource to engineers – and not just IT types. A good PI remembers what it's like to be an entity of flesh, blood, bone and a scant dollop of brains.

It's time the technical professions recognized the importance of including incompetents on their team. We are here to help. Our incapacity is fathomless. We know how to do it wrong. We can misunderstand, misapply, mishandle, mishear, misread, misconstrue, misconceive, miscalculate and, God knows, mistake. Our product is incompetence, the gift that keeps on giving.

A good PI's incompetence goes beyond computers. We can also point out the inadequacies of assembly instructions that involve little pictures rather than words. We've got the words, verbal redundancies to the tune of "Don't be stupid. There are big screws and little screws. The big screws go in the big holes. The little screws go in the little holes. Turn the screws clockwise with a screwdriver (fig. 1). The little holes should be on your left. If they're on your right, you're holding it upside down. Don't lose the screws."

We PIs need to form a trade association and get ourselves certified. Trouble is, none of us know how to do such a thing. And anybody who knows how is too smart to understand the fundamentals of idiocy. Their brilliance is an incompetence.

I'm not going to wait for some clown to invent a Certified Professional Idiot exam. I'm going to gut my résumé of skills, most of which were lies anyway. I'm going to replace them with a list of every dumb thing I've ever done, from buying a banana farm to opening a store in downtown New London.

And the time I ran for public office. Fortunately, the electorate recognized the incipient threat of idiocracy, and they mostly voted for the other guy. Political leaders who want to better understand what it takes to lose can hire me as consultant.

If my new consultancy works as well as I expect, I may be able to retire someday. Maybe I'll go back to that banana farm and try again.

Dog Tale

A few years ago I set out to steal a dog.
    I knew this was a felony. It wouldn't be my first. I'm guilty of a few others. Most were of an adolescent nature. Some were more ambitious, such as "Conspiracy to Overthrow the Government of the United States."

Let me hasten to add that I've never been convicted.

The dog plot was different. It wasn't theft as much as liberation. It was a situation where the law didn't apply.

I knew her as Woofie (not her real name) because that's all she ever said to me. Not a big woof. It was a gentle, muffled woof without conviction or emotional involvement.

Woofie was an old spaniel. She lived 24/7/365 on a chain. She could walk about ten feet from her little house to the far end of the overhead cable. Then she could walk back.

She was out there alone all day, all night, all summer, all winter. Nobody loved Woofie.

Her house was off to the side of a big white house occupied by an elderly couple. When I passed Woofie's house on my evening walks, she'd give me an obligatory woof. She had little worth guarding, no investment in the big white house. One woof sufficed.

I often stopped to talk with Woofie, give her a little pet and some words of sympathy. Sometimes I brought her a morsel of leftovers.

Then I took to unhooking her chain. Suddenly free, she'd dart away, stubby tail all a'wiggle, nose to the ground, sucking up the world that had always been so close yet impossibly far.

Is unhooking a dog a crime? I suppose I should have consulted an attorney, but I didn't.

Woofie never disappeared for long. In some sad sense of loyalty, I guess, she must have ended up at the door of the big white house. The next day, she was always back on her chain. I'd release her again, to her repeated delight.

Then one day I found the clip on her chain was welded shut. This was the first sign that maybe somebody actually wanted Woofie. It scared me a bit. But I pulled the collar over her head anyway.

Along came winter. Woofie looked depressed and dispirited, not shivering but panting out clouds of icy breath. Sometimes she stayed curled up in her little house. I could have burglarized the big white house without her giving a woof.

It was too cold. I decided to steal Woofie, take her home, give her a soft bed in a warm house.

Despite my criminal past, I was very nervous about this operation. It was going to be a little complicated. I'd have to make the snatch, then walk my furry pelf for a nearly a mile back to my house.

This was no longer a matter of mischief or misdemeanor. I was entering the domain of larceny, or even, if Woofie had papers, grand larceny. Regardless of my humane intentions, if caught I could find myself in a situation not unlike Woofie's.

I needed moral support. I enlisted a couple of accomplices, dog-loving hold-my-beer types not much more mature than me. One, in fact, could serve as a worst-case-scenario attorney, should one become necessary, though not until he got out of law school.

Armed with collar and leash, we approached under cover of darkness at approximately dinnertime. My accomplices deployed to stations up and down the road. No, we didn't have lampblack on our faces, but it sure felt like it.

I crept in for the release. Woofie was sure glad to see me, though she seemed suspicious. His collar was tighter than usual.

Then, suddenly, a neighbor opened her back door and started whistling and screaming into the dark. She seemed to be calling her own dog, but that wasn't certain.

In a harsh whisper my attorney, justifiably concerned about being arrested right before taking his Bar exam, shouted, "Abort mission! Repeat, abort mission!"

And so we did. We scrambled back where we'd come from to debrief and alleviate the thirst we'd built up.

For several days I avoided the scene of the unconsummated crime. But eventually I felt I had to go back and do some explaining.

But Woofie was gone.

I have no idea what happened to her. A few months later, the big white house was sold. I have no idea what happened to the two old people. Both accomplices got jobs and moved away. Only I remain to tell the tale.

Testing Teachers

My beloved sister was cruel enough to send me a little package— a flashback of my life in disparate artifacts—letters I'd sent from South America, a photo of me in a canoe, newspaper clippings that mentioned my name, my high school diploma, shoulder patches representing things that I used to care about.

The painful part was a collection of report cards going back more than half a century.

The arrival of report cards was always a moment of hope and dread—the hope of excellence, the dread of failure, the likelihood of continued mediocrity.

The oldest came from the first grade, signed by a teacher—Viola Crispell—I'm sad to say I've forgotten. She found me "satisfactory" across the board. (Satisfactory was as good as you could get. Excellence was not an option.) Apparently I followed simple directions, strove for good posture, and made use of a handkerchief.

I don't remember Mrs. Crispell, but I do remember why I was absent for 23 and a half days. It was measles and chicken pox. But thanks to a vaccine made available just the year before, I was spared polio.

By the fourth grade, satisfactory was slipping from my grasp. Mr. McCormack was so tall—nearly 20 feet—that he couldn't read my handwriting. That might also explain why he thought I was a lousy speller. He might be pleased to know I've improved in both skills, though not a lot.

I don't know who the art teacher was, but she found me only "fair" at art. She recognized my originality but thought I sucked at expression.

Hello, Mrs. Art Teacher? Maybe I sucked at expression because your idea of an art lesson was to tell us to paint our favorite animal, not HOW to paint our favorite animal. That's why I painted a duck. Not because I have a thing for ducks but because I thought I could paint one.

Turned out I couldn't. Was that my fault or yours?

Next time (we get to do life again, right?), you're getting a picture of a worm.

Fifth grade: the lovely Mrs. Lawrence, a veritable grandmother of love. After lunch she used to turn off the lights and read us a book. She believed I could do advanced work. She had nothing to do with my "Fair—needs improvement" in not just art but music.

Hello, Mrs. Music Teacher? How badly was I singing "I've Been Working on the Railroad"? If you were actually teaching anything, I missed it. I still can't read music.

Sixth grade: Mr. Henriquez, who taught me to hate school. The "Good" I earned the first semester–baggage from Mrs. Lawrence–deteriorated to multiple counts of "Needs Improvement." I didn't strive to do my best. I didn't apply social skills consistently. I needed to be more careful. I didn't hand in assignments on time.

He recommended I not be allowed to take Band in junior high school. I still can't play an instrument, am still notoriously careless, still have trouble with those social skills.

High school: the struggle to attain average. Art teachers who taught me that art cannot be learned. Gym teachers who eradicated any interest in sports. A shop teacher who let me plane one side of one board for 12 weeks, and confirmed my certainty that I couldn't do anything right. A Spanish teacher who said she felt sorry for me. A geometry teacher who cared and coaxed. A writing teacher I loved.

We all remember the teachers who cared and tried and inspired, though I don't recall ever expressing gratitude except maybe with a flash of understanding in my eyes.

And we remember the teachers who let us down, who failed to teach, "fair" at best, needing improvement, lacking effort and below average.

This fall, we put our teachers to the test. We need to respect their courage and dedication, to cut them all due slack. We–all of us–need to help them as our good teachers helped us in the past.

Let Restaurants Restore

I'm not one to complain about food. I'll eat just about anything except insects, testicles, squid brain, and beets.

On the other hand, I can easily go a day without food if there's nothing worth eating. If the choice is hunger or something shrouded in a condom of cellophane, I can wait without complaint..

I'm more likely to complain about a restaurant. Before I do so, let me point out that once I ate at an eatery on the outskirts of Ouagadougou where six or so strangers and I shared not only a table but a single tomato sauce can of water dipped from a rusty barrel. But I did not complain. The place was quiet, unpretentious and cheap.

I mention this because, as the quarantine loosens, we are being urged to go out to eat, to contribute to a last-minute rescue of a small local business.

I'm all for local business, be it in suburban Ouagadougou or downtown New London. Spending money at a local place (as opposed to a local franchise) is more like sharing than actually committing an expenditure.

But restauranteurs beware: I like to cook, and I'd rather chop my own vegetables than pay $50 to be annoyed for an hour.

What annoys me? Waiter, the whine list, please!

For starters: television. I've seen televisions in restaurants, but I've never seen anyone actually watching. The glittery slime creeping from the TV set distracts the eye, but to what end? The only good thing about restaurant TV is that the sound is usually turned off. So why is it there?

Speaking of sound, who picked your music? The busboy? Is it appropriate for dancing? I ask because I've never seen people dance in a restaurant. That's not what they're there for.

Let me suggest the music be appropriate to the atmosphere. Thai food? Thai music. Classy food? Classy music. Testicles and squid brain? Punk.

Whatever it is, keep it soft. In the background. Loud music makes people talk loud, and loud people make people holler. People aren't there for the music. It isn't a concert or a shouting match.

And here's another thing: I will agree to chew with my mouth shut and keep my elbows off the table if the waitstaff will refrain from interrupting me to ask if everything's okay.

Unless I'm holding my throat with two hands and turning blue, the question's probably best left unasked. Since everything (well, almost everything) was okay until the question was asked, you don't want to hear the answer. Rather than listen to me rant about the television, the music and the beets that I specifically requested be substituted with onion rings, staff would do better to go see if there's soap, towels and hot water in the restroom.

Let me suggest something else. A tablecloth. Cloth napkins. A flower. A candle. Big pluses for a small expense. If the party's check is going to exceed $50, why not jack it up by a few bucks to make the table inviting and pleasant? It's what distinguishes a real restaurant from a fast-food trough.

Enough with the gripes. Let me speak in praise of outdoor dining and sidewalk bars. Why did we need a pandemic to give us the courage to do what Europeans have been doing since summer was invented?

I hope someone does a study of how outdoor dining has impacted urban life. What got worse? Crime? Public drunkenness? Juvenile delinquency? Litter?

It may turn out that the only downside is the hubbub of clinking glasses and people enjoying themselves. If so, we'll have to ask ourselves what was stopping us from doing this all along.

The word "restaurant" comes from a French verb, "restaurer" – to restore. A "restaurant" is literally "that which restores." Restaurants restore personal energy, community spirits, and local economies. I look forward to eating "out" this summer.

Ambulance Writer

The recent Day article on ambulance heroes brought back memories of my stint on the local ambulance. I was a volunteer Emergency Medical Technician, a professional status somewhere between a medic and a boy scout with a merit badge.

Other than getting jerked awake by a beeper in the middle of the night and having to drive off into the winter dark, I didn't see it as especially heroic. I was just helping out.

My perspective on the experience was more of mental challenge than heroics. Every call was different. One never knew what to expect. Humans get into all sorts of painful situations. The variety of human ailments goes way beyond the knowledge of any EMT. A call for chest pains might turn out to be a gall bladder on the fritz. The reported nose bleed might be the result of domestic violence. There might be a crime in progress. There might be a dog.

And then there's the challenge of figuring what to do. The EMT's responsibility is mostly a matter of transportation. But in occasional cases, some kind of treatment is necessary. Stop the bleeding. Immobilize the bone. Put ice on it. Fifteen liters of oxygen per minute, chest compressions just about as fast as you can go.

The back of the ambulance is an ad libbed orchestra of activity. It's real team work. No plan at the outset. No leader giving orders. Everybody looking for what needs to be done. List the meds. Keep an eye on the blood pressure. Monitor patient's coherence. Get the bag valve mask. Call in the trauma. Write a report. Mop up.

This being an ambulance operation, it all happens quickly. No lingering conversations. No hanging around. No hugs and handshakes upon departure. We package the patient—yes, that's the verb—and make haste for a hospital. Patient's choice: L&M, Backus, or Windham. We're back at the station within the hour.

It takes a while to calm down. There's no going back to sleep. To decelerate, I wrote down notes on the call—what happened, what we found, how the patient felt about the problem, and what I'd done wrong.

I always did something wrong. I never did a perfect call. This disturbed me. Sooner or later I was going to hurt somebody. But as one EMT (who was also a nurse) told me, the worst thing you can do to them is do nothing.

The work challenged my intellect and satisfied my compulsion to help. But in another way, it ran against my professional tendencies. I write for a living.

Writing may be the only activity where one is supposed to get it wrong the first time. As on an ambulance, the practitioner dives into a situation without knowing much about it. Unlike the EMT, however, the writer gets to linger and look around, notice telling details, and hammer out a first draft just to see how it looks, then see what treatment it needs and how to make it better.

The second shot ends up in the trash, too. Maybe the third draft needs no more than moving the end up to the beginning, the beginning back to the middle somewhere, and the insertion of a telling detail or two. Maybe start over again.

The waste basket is a writer's best friend.

That approach doesn't work on an ambulance call. There's no experimentation. No creative solutions. No second-draft do-over. Just because chest pain may lead to chest compressions, you can't try elbow compressions on a broken arm. You don't get to see if it works, then try something else. You have to get it right the first time. There's no waste basket.

I got out of ambulance work before I hurt somebody. But when I hear that siren go by in the middle of the night, I remember hanging off a grab-bar while hooking up an oxygen line, my right arm doing the work of a doctor, my left arm the work of an ape. I remember some of the lessons I learned. I apply them with a pen to paper, trying hard not to hurt anyone, and trying to get it right.

Failure is Good for You

Failure—the gift that keeps on giving.

It's painful. It's embarrassing. It follows you, even becomes you, if not in the memory of others, then in your own.

Failure's like a mistake, yet so much more. It's even more than a set of mistakes. It's more like a set of mistakes you made an effort to accomplish, mistakes adding up to a painful punchline: you should have known better.

We have plenty of synonyms and euphemisms for fail and failure, each with its own nuance: Blunder. Losing. Worst-case scenario. Unintended consequences. Fubar, flubs, flops and major flops. Catastrophic failures. Epic failures that make history. Cascading failures that cause failures that cause failures.

"Fail-safe" is a thing, but as soon as we hear the word, we know what's going to happen.

Funny how there's such a thing as a qualified success but not a qualified failure.

It used to be an event. The dam that failed. The plot that failed. The company, the invasion, the Roget's motion, the brakes that failed.

But at some point in recent history, failure expanded to become an existential character trait, as in "He was a failure as a shortstop," or "She's a failure as a mother."

Yet you never hear, "She was a failure as a beagle." Dogs may fail to do a job— fail to find the body, fail to bite the burglar—but we never extend the failure to define the dog's inner being. Maybe it's because we consider them failures from the get-go, human wannabes who manage to love, cry, sit, stay, beg and rejoice but can't quite succeed at tying their own shoes or running for public office. They can chase the mailman—bad dog!—but we don't blame them if they can't deliver the mail.

I've done some hands-on research into failure, and I've achieved some success at it. Farming in Brazil. Teaching Spanish in middle school. Running around Manhattan in a three-piece suit. Painting a picture of a horse. I even tried running for public office.

I've enjoyed failure upon failure upon failure with intermittent worst-case scenarios and unintended consequences as I flopped and blundered my way through the dismal Swamp of Snafu. But I'm still here, ready to blow it again.

So I'd like to take a fresh look at failure.

Maybe failure's a good thing, something to be proud of. Unmitigated success is merely a sign that somebody failed to strive for something greater. Anyone who has never failed has failed to learn something very important about life. They also missed out on a lot of fun.

Failure, in fact, is a fundamental trait of humanity. Look how we've been blundering along! Somehow it seems like that's all humanity ever does. And somehow here we are, ready to blow it again.

But all those failures were really the result of people trying to make things better, better than they could actually achieve. And the successes have usually been nothing more than successfully causing someone else to fail.

And how many successes–personal, social, historical–were built on the lessons of previous failures? Had we failed to fail, we'd never have succeeded.

And how often has success bred failure? I'm looking at you, Pope Gregory IX, you and your "Vox in Rama" bull of 1233, the one where you declared cats to be creatures of the devil working in cahoots with witches. So the faithful across Christendom killed every cat they could find. The massacre was largely a success, which may explain the subsequent public health failure known as the bubonic plague. Next thing you know, one in three Europeans was dead. Good job, Greg! Way to go!

Romanian philosopher Emil Cioran suggested we embrace failure. Every failure, he said, teaches us something. Our reaction to it tests our character. Anyone who isn't failing isn't trying. In fact, they aren't even fully human.

And what tells us more about a person—success or failure? Success proves nothing but competence at a level of achievability. Failure might tell us about overconfidence, but they also tell us about values, courage and dreams.

I've never met anyone truly interested in my income or a game I won. But when I mention my banana farm or doing battle with a room full of middle-schoolers, they're interested. It's as if they're interested in me. The real me. The failure who's still here.

Looking Back

Life Aboard the Mayflower

As the repaired and refurbished Mayflower II plies the seas off New London, let us remember her ancestor, the one that brought 102 immigrants from Plymouth to Plymouth in 1620.

The Mayflower was a "high-pooped pot-bellied merchantman." That's about all we know about her. Her descendant was built on conjecture and surmise.

Her pot-belly was a midriff bulge at her waterline. It kept her from rocking too much in calm waters. It also kept her from slicing through the water. When she sailed, she lurched forward a few feet, then settled down, then lurched again.

On August 15, two Pilgrim ships—the Mayflower and the Speedwell, shoved off from Southampton. Within 300 miles, it became apparent that the Speedwell had been poorly named. The only thing she did well was leak.

The ships returned to Dartmouth (at the mouth of the River Dart) for repairs. Then they tried again. Same problem. They went back, putting in at Plymouth, where it was decided that the Speedwell would never make it across the Atlantic.

Goods and passengers were shuffled over to the Mayflower and packed in tight. The 102 passengers were berthed on the gun deck, a dark, low space between the main deck and the hold.

They shared about 1,800 square feet with a 30' boat, at least a couple of cannons, piles of carry-on luggage, bilge pumps, spare parts, the base of the masts, the capstan, a couple of dogs and a few small farm animals. With pathways kept clear for crew, each passenger was left with less than the space of a single bed.

On September 16, they lurched westward into hurricane season. They enjoyed a few days of "prosperous winds," but then things turned rough with "boisterous storms."

A boisterous storm could tilt the ship across an arc of 90 degrees in a matter of seconds. Waves lifted and dropped the ship by 80' or more. As waves washed across the deck, water trickled down on the passengers.

In the windowless space, the passengers could not align their balance with the horizon. Seasickness overwhelmed them. We can only imagine the scene as they heaved up pea porridge, oatmeal, beer-soaked biscuits and bits of salted cod.

The closest thing to a bathroom was the "head," an enclosed space at water-level up at the bow. It had a slatted floor so waves could gush up and wash away the waste. (This was not the poop deck. The poop deck was the roof above the captain's quarters at the stern.)

Three passengers were pregnant. One gave birth and named her baby Oceanus. His first meal probably tasted of seawater.

At one point a wave punched the Mayflower so hard that a stout oak beam snapped as loud as a rifle shot. This beam held the main deck up and the hull out. Within a few moments another wave might finish the job.

As the ship rose and fell and tossed side to side, water poured in and men scrambled in the dark to find a house jack. Miraculously, they managed to secure the beam.

Master Jones owned and commanded the ship as it tacked into the westerlies. His navigation instruments were no more than a magnetized sliver of iron, a jar of sand, a couple of sticks with marked measurements, and a long piece of rope. His progress, lurch after lurch, was about two miles per hour.

Jones was aiming at someplace just south of the Hudson, the northern edge of Virginia. On November 19, someone high in the rigging probably shouted "Land ho!" as they sighted Cape Cod. It was a close miss, just half of one degree north of the Hudson.

It was close enough for the passengers. For reasons no one knows, they decided to disembark there rather than in Virginia, where they had permission to settle. On November 21, the Mayflower dropped anchor inside the curl of the cape.

Thus ended the easy part of the trip. It was too late to plant crops or dig the frozen soil Also too late for a ship to cross the Atlantic. The passengers spent the winter in their dank gun deck space. By spring, almost half had died of disease.

On April 15, the Mayflower sailed out of Plymouth Harbor. All the Pilgrims remained. If there was a moment they became Americans, that was it.

Why the Pilgrims Are the Ones We Remember

Once again, though in many cases in smaller numbers than past years, families across country will come together today to share a bounty of food and bow their heads in a moment of thankfulness.

To a mostly symbolic extent, we will emulate the Pilgrim experience of 1621. We'll invite friends. We'll eat the same kind of bird those settlers shared with their Pokonoket neighbors. We'll eat squash and beans and pumpkin pie. We'll decorate our homes with silly icons of settlers, blunderbusses, turkeys, Native Americans, and a ship called Mayflower.

The Thanksgiving feast is better appreciated if we understand that the Pilgrims were not the first to bow their heads in thanks before a meal. Settlers at Jamestown had done so more than a decade before the Pilgrims. Spanish settlers had done so a hundred years before that.

So why do we venerate the Pilgrims of Plymouth?

We have good reason. The Plymouth and Jamestown experiences were radically different. Only one became the paragon of America.

The settlers who founded Jamestown in 1607 were mostly men who planned to get rich off furs, tobacco, and gold, then return to England. They did not come to stay, and they did not bring their families.

Many of them were "gentlemen" who had no intention of actually working. They tried to talk the local people, the Powhatan, into doing the work. When the Powhatan declined the job offer, the English tried to force them.

Force didn't work. It devolved into torture, murder, and war. The Powhatan surrounded Jamestown and tried to starve the inhabitants. They almost succeeded, and some of the English resorted to cannibalism.

The Pilgrims had a different approach. They came as families, and they came to stay. They were working-class people who were not afraid to get their hands dirty.

Not that they had an easy time of it. They arrived in mid-November. They had to spend the winter aboard the ship. A respiratory disease hit them hard. Forty-five of the 102 passengers died.

That spring, when Pokonoket warriors threatened the village, the settlers made one of the most crucial decisions in the history of America. Rather than fire off a few preemptory shots to show how tough they were, a few brave men went outside the stockade and made a show of laying their weapons down.

It was a beautiful gesture of Christian goodwill. And it worked. The Pokonoket sachem, Massasoit, dared come to talk. The two peoples not only reached certain agreements but recognized each other's humanity.

The Pokonoket and Pilgrims – the natives and immigrants – became friends. The immigrants dug in, built houses, and planted crops. By autumn, they had something to celebrate and be thankful for.

So, they declared a Day of Thanksgiving and prepared a harvest feast. Along came the Pokonoket, and of course they were invited to share the bounty. More than a hundred guests stayed for a three-day feast. Despite differences in language and customs, they all got along.

That is why we emulate the Plymouth experience, not Jamestown. We celebrate the bounty, the goodwill, the friendship, and life itself. Those are the seeds of the American culture. We grew from that.

At our house, before we bow for grace on Thanksgiving, I read this paragraph from a book I wrote:

"The Mayflower contained a cross-section of values that would become quintessentially American: the insistence on following the heart rather than the law; the inability to tolerate injustice; the audacity to demand authority over authorities; the courage to pursue a better life no matter how much worse it might be; the wisdom of working together as a society for mutual benefit and personal profit. They believed in the power of the congregation. They would do their own thinking and make their own decisions. They would pray their own prayers. They would dig in their heels. The strong would bury the weak, perhaps suffer a moment of doubt, then remember the mercy of their God, and then get back to work."

The Pilgrims: Sloppy, Lucky, and Smart

In 1620, the people we call the Pilgrims did something incredibly foolish. They packed themselves into a dank, overcrowded space on a ship called Mayflower and set sail for a distant world. As happens in any untried venture, they made many mistakes. But they got the fundamentals right, and with a dollop of luck – or call it divine providence – they accomplished the impossible.

Their mistakes would seem to doom the venture. They leased the Mayflower – smart move – but they also bought a ship called the Speedwell. But the only thing the Speedwell did well was leak. After two midsummer attempts to sail west, they gave up on the Speedwell. They packed 102 men, women, and children into the Mayflower, and on September 16 shoved off for good.

Big mistake. It would take two months to reach the New World. It would be snowing by the time they arrived, way too late to plant crops and a difficult time to build houses. What were they thinking?

They weren't thinking about hurricane season, which is what they were sailing into. They hit a few storms, one of which was no place for a wooden ship. A wave hit them broadside so hard it cracked a stout oak beam. One more hit and the ship would crack in half. But by luck, working in pitch dark in a lurching ship, they found a house jack and forced the beam back into position.

They were aiming for someplace just south of the Hudson but arrived just north of Cape Cod – not bad for a navigator working with just a couple of sticks, a long piece of string, and a sliver of magnetized iron. For reasons unknown, they decided to settle there instead of down south. Maybe they expected weather like that of balmy Barcelona, which was just as far north.

If so, they were wrong. Snow was falling, the ground frozen. They had to spend the winter aboard the ship. Packed hip-to-hip in the windowless deck, they infected each other with a respiratory disease. By February, almost half had died.

They ran out of beer. Food ran short. Then they discovered that someone had forgotten to pack the fishhooks. Hunting was tough because their firearms depended on smoldering hemp. Wandering the woods in a cloud of cannabis smoke, they had trouble finding game.

And then, in March, suddenly, just outside the settlement, local people started shouting and brandishing bows and arrows. The settlers had to make a big decision – to fire off a preemptive volley to scare off the "savages," or, in Christian and political wisdom, offer goodwill. If they made the wrong decision, they'd be dead Pilgrims.

A few men went outside the palisade and laid their weapons on the ground. There they stood, as brave as men but vulnerable as babes. The locals understood the gesture. They approached unarmed. The mutual goodwill allowed the Pokanoket and the English to become good friends.

And then — talk about luck! — along came a local who spoke fluent English, the man we know as Squanto. Squanto had already been across the Atlantic four times. Arriving the last time, he found his entire tribe, the Patuxet, dead of disease. Everyone figured the land was cursed. Nobody wanted it. If the English chose to settle there, nobody cared. Bad mistakes resulted in the deaths of half the Pilgrims. Dumb luck helped the rest survive. But it was fundamental values that allowed Plymouth to thrive. The Pilgrims had come as families. They had come to work and build new lives, not get rich quick off gold, slaves, or conquest. They took their Christianity seriously, achieving peace through goodwill. They stuck together. They promoted the general welfare. They planted the seeds that grew into a nation. This is what we remember on Thanksgiving. For this we still give thanks.

Let Them Eat Cake

Once upon a time an election was a very special event. It was worthy of celebration. But it wasn't a celebration of who won. It was a celebration that leaders had been chosen by the people, not a king.

In Connecticut, such a celebration took place as votes were counted at the old State House in Hartford. People came together from all over. They wore their best. The governor arrived with a military entourage and gubernatorial horses. There were an election sermon, an election choir, a grand election ball, lots of food and more than a modicum of booze.

The food came to include something called Hartford Election Cake. The recipes varied but had an identifiable commonality. For one thing, they were big. They were meant to feed not family but community. People milled around the State House with baskets of cake to offer to friends and strangers. In other words, it wasn't just cake. It was community, democracy and pride in the possibility of rule by the ruled. It was ritual, a high-calorie mouthful of "We did it again!"

Elections were extra special in Connecticut. The state was proud to have had elections since 1662, when King Charles II gave Connecticut a Royal Charter. It gave Connecticut the right to make its own laws and elect its own leaders. It was the Charter that ended up hidden in the Charter Oak.

It was a ponderous cake. A recipe in a women's magazine in 1863 called for nine pounds of flour, nine pounds of butter, 10 eggs, three pints of yeast, nine pounds of brown sugar, lots of nutmeg, cinnamon and mace, nine pounds of raisins, eight wine glasses of sherry and just as much brandy.

And it was a complicated cake. Recipes often included long instructions, beginning with how to make the yeast. It would have to rise overnight twice. If milk was right out of the cow, it was warm enough; otherwise, it needed to be heated up. But not too much lest the butter turn oily.

As people migrated westward and up the Connecticut River, they took their cookbooks. As the tradition spread, "Hartford" grew moot. The cake became known as simply Election Cake.

The tradition faded a bit as women (i.e. the cooks) joined the workforce, immigrants introduced new foods, and communities became less cohesive. The Election Cakes got smaller and the recipes called for less alcohol.

The tradition has not, however, died. An internet search for "election cake recipe" turns up over 8,000 results.

What has died, however, is the celebratory nature of elections. We still manage to do it, but if there's a celebration, it's over a winner, not the cherished process.

The recent polarization of politics has further robbed us of the communal nature of democracy. It's hard to imagine people of all persuasions coming together outside town hall not to say "We won!" but "We did it!"

Connecticut State Historian Walter Woodward wants to change that. He says the Election Cake could be a recipe for a more cooperative democracy and communal community.

"We all feel something's not right today, that something's gone wrong," Woodward said in a recent podcast. "What might be the bridge that brings us back together is to agree that the right to cast a vote and choose the people who rule is something to celebrate."

Hence the Election Day Cake Virtual Contest, organized by the Connecticut Democracy Center at the Old State House. Since the judging has to be done virtually – thank you, Mr. Coronavirus – it's a contest of cake decoration, not recipe. Results will be announced tomorrow.

Cake just might get us through these stressful times.

"We need civil discourse to take center stage again," Woodward says. "If we can just get people to sit down and eat some cake with someone whose views we don't agree with, as long as we don't end up throwing cake at each other, we can probably learn something."

Little Bucket of Miscellany

Some Fates of Cats

I've been worried about the homeless cats hunkering at the Connecticut Humane Society in Quaker Hill. Are they languishing in quarantine like a bunch of New Yorkers in tiny apartments, no one to scratch their chinny-chin-chins?

Yes and no. Many have found local foster homes for the duration, and the rest are languishing in the Society's Newington facility. They'll be back in Quaker Hill someday, though nobody knows when.

But cats are good at languishing. And when they get tired of it, they take a nap.

Really, they have it pretty easy. History has not been kind to homeless cats. Here are some cases of cats colliding with technology in the late 20th century.

The Cat Bomb

In one of the most indubitably stupid ideas in the history of mankind, someone thought of using a cat to make a rudimentary smart bomb.

This was back during World War II. Bombs were pretty dumb back then. Despite the supposed accuracy of the Norden bombsight, bombardiers were finding it hard to hit a moving ship with a moving bomb dropped from a moving airplane.

Some idiot's solution: put a cat inside the bomb and connect its paws to flaps that would guide the bomb.

The idiot's theory: If cats hate water and always land on their feet, then a cat in a bomb with a window would make the movements necessary to land on the ship instead of in the ocean.

The fatal flaw: among the many flaws in this plan—actually, it's hard to think of any part of the plan that isn't a flaw—is the fact that the cat would need to practice. But this was a suicide mission. Whether the bomb hit the ship or the ocean, the cat would not get a second chance.

Only one cat bomb was built and deployed. It missed its target. History knows nothing about the cat—neither name nor type nor age. Nor do we have any idea what thoughts may have gone through its head as the bomb tilted out the bomb bay and fell toward the ocean and a tiny ship way down there.

Cats in Space

Dogs were flying into outer space ten years before cats. Soviet rockets shot nine dogs into space between 1950 and 1951. Some went alone. Some went in pairs. Some lived. Some didn't. Three went twice. One lucky dog escaped, presumably in the direction of the Berlin Wall.

It wasn't until 1963 that a homeless black and white Parisian feline, Félicette, boldly went where no Frenchman had gone before, though three French mice had been launched to see if space flight was safe for cats.

Félicette went through two months of training before her flight. One exercise involved being swung around in a three-axis chair on a centrifuge while hearing the roar of a rocket taking off.

Among six cats deemed qualified for space flight, Félicette was chosen to go first because she was cool. Packed into a capsule atop a Véronique rocket, Félicette was shot 94 miles above the Sahara Desert. Electrodes implanted in her brain detected that she was "vigilant" during the experience. She experienced five minutes of weightlessness before parachuting safely to earth.

Enthused by the success of the flight, the French tried to send another cat into space, but something went wrong on the launch. The fate of the other cats is not known. Félicette remains the only cat to have survived space travel.

The Cloak-and-Dagger Cat

Another stupid idea involving a cat. During the cold war, the CIA trained a cat, code-named Acoustic Kitty, to sneak into the Soviet Union embassy with a microphone. (The cat's real name is still classified.)

The microphone was implanted in the cat. As a CIA officer described it, "They slit the cat open, put batteries in him, and wired him up...The tail was used as an antenna. They made a monstrosity."

Training the cat went about as well as you might expect. It took five years. The whole project cost $10 million.

Finally a van packed with electronics released the secret agent outside the Soviet embassy. Free at last, it ran into the street and got run over by a taxi.

"There they were," the CIA officer reported, "sitting in the van with all those dials, and the cat was dead."

This piece appeared in The Day on April 3, 2005
following a news article on a mock terrorist
attack to be staged in New London.

Mock This

You want to mock a terrorist attack? Mock this: The terrorists are already in the gates. Nobody knows who they are. They look like elected officials, celebrities on TV, students in school, executives with briefcases, dudes hanging out on street corners.

With an ingenious distribution system, they scatter 192 million guns in American homes. No one knows who has them. The plan works. Two hundred thousand people get shot in a year. Thirty thousand die. Five thousand are children. In fact, some of the gunmen are actually gunchildren, kids gone mad with a rage beyond our understanding. The president, confused but resolved, does nothing.

A band of terrorists breaks into the national treasury, empties the whole thing, leaves a hole in the bottom so deep it will take two generations to plug it up. They send the almighty dollar into a tailspin around the deep, dark drain of depression. Nobody notices.

They rob the poor and give to the rich. They pull a fast one on the elderly, trick the unborn out of their pensions, saddle them with federal debt. They leave children behind. They bait. They switch. They cover their tracks.

They use lies and innuendo to draw our army to the other side of the world. They make killing into a Christian virtue. They beg for the apocalypse. They post ten commandments and break them one by one. They hang with a bad crowd.

Look out. Here they come. Code Orange! Code Orange! Please remove your shoes.

With our soldiers tied down in a distant desert, dying like fish in a barrel, terrorists continue their rampage in American streets, schools, homes, parks, post offices, courthouses. Students shoot teachers. Criminals execute judges. Parents beat their children. Children kill their parents. Neighbors rape neighbors, leave their bodies in the woods.

The terrorists slay national forests, dig pits in national parks, cast oil upon the waters. They release gases to the sky, chemicals to the streams, toxins over the crops. They poison wells. They push narcotics on the young. They withhold medicine from the old. They make cancer happen.

While televisions gush with glitz and idiocy, the terrorists throw journalists in jail. They make a bad journalist a whore. They make a whore a bad journalist. They let him into the White House. He asks stupid questions, gets stupid answers. He does not remove his shoes.

They slash the Constitution, seize without need, search without warrant, arrest without cause, hold without charges, try without jury, and outsource cruel and unusual punishment to places where tyranny rules.

They rule. They corrupt. They buy legislators. They sell favors. They puff themselves up on TV but fling so much mud that nobody can see what's happening. They replace voting machines with black boxes. Nobody gets to look inside. They fool enough of the people enough of the time.

The president lifts his chin, wrinkles his brow, squints his eyes, raises his arm, waves with courage, gets in his helicopter, leaves.

It's all too horrible to think about, but that's the attack that's happening. We can mock an assault on Fort Trumbull, rehearse it all we want, but it won't stop what truly terrorizes, not one little bit.

Peace On Earth, Goodbye To Subs

As we celebrate the birth of Jesus, we would do well to consider his likely opinion of nuclear submarines. Since our region produces so many of these incredibly deadly weapons, we owe it to Jesus to think about what we are doing.

As U.S. Rep. Rob Simmons calls on the government to fund the building of more submarines than the Navy feels it needs, we should reflect on the wisdom and Christianity of such expenditures.

It was the prophet Isaiah who suggested beating swords into ploughshares and spears into pruning hooks, but it was Jesus, the prince of peace, who took the idea further. He advised us to love our enemies, turn the other cheek, and do unto others as we'd have them do unto us.

It's hard to figure how Groton's weapons of mass destruction fit in with that philosophy.

Even people hell-bent on war should realize the stupidity of dedicating huge amounts of money to the building of nuclear submarines. We no longer have enemies that can be held off with the threat of mass annihilation. The submarines we had on Sept. 11, 2001, failed to protect us. More submarines won't help at all.

In fact it could be argued that the military approach to world peace isn't working. Despite our gargantuan power, and the global reach of our high-tech swords, we get into war after war after war. The current wars, in fact, seem to be caused by a reaction to our imposition of power where it isn't wanted.

The power of our submarines isn't helping us wage war in Afghanistan or Iraq. Our soldiers there aren't getting killed and mutilated for lack of submarines. They're suffering for lack of simple armor.

Too many of them are hoping to get Kevlar in their Christmas stockings. And too many other people are hoping to give them shrapnel.

Alas, in a statement as anti-Christmas as "Bah, humbug," our secretary of Defense tells us we can't have the army we'd like to have. Even though we spend almost as much on our military as the entire rest of the world, we can't afford the basic equipment that saves lives. We can't even stand up against an impoverished, leaderless, army-less country like Iraq.

It makes you wonder where our tax dollars have gone.

One place they've gone is into submarines.

When Rep. Simmons returns to Washington after Christmas, he will take with him two conflicting interests. One is that thousands of his constituents are employed in the building of submarines. The other is that tens of thousands of his constituents have celebrated Christmas because they believe in the teachings of Christ. They believe that love works, that we're better off investing in ploughshares than in swords.

If Mr. Simmons is the good leader he claims to be, and presumably one who celebrated Christmas, perhaps he can give some thought to resolving that conflict between Christian values and employment in the weapons industry.

Maybe Jesus and Isaiah have already offered him the solution. Why don't we employ people in the building of ploughshares rather than submarines? Why don't we build machines that produce energy rather than machines that produce, at best, if we're lucky, nothing? Why don't we offer our enemies (and the rest of the world) something nice rather than something deadly?

Christmas would be a nice time to think about whether Jesus was right and to notice how poorly submarines fit under a proper Christmas tree. Our swords have not brought the world peace. We really should be thinking about building something else.

About the Author

Glenn Alan Cheney is a writer, translator, painter, and managing editor of New London Librarium. He is the author of more than 30 books on such disparate topics as Chernobyl, Brazil's Quilombo dos Palmares, the Estrada Real, nuns, death and burial, eschatology, cats, bees, incarceration, the Pilgrims, Abraham Lincoln, nuclear proliferation, and the testing of atomic bombs. He also writes poetry and fiction. He translates Brazilian classics from Portuguese to English. He has written articles, op-eds and columns for several newspapers. He lives in Hanover, Conn., with his wife, Solange Aurora.

New London Librarium

New London Librarium is a boutique press specializing in books that merit publication but are unlikely to yield the sales required by larger publishers. Series include Catholic issues, the environment, Brazil, art, history, and fiction. For more information, see NLLibrarium.com.

Made in the USA
Columbia, SC
19 December 2021

52037160R00159